FEDERAL LAW S
FOR MPJE

ALL TOPICS IN THE EXAM BLUEPRINT

Written Material for the RxPrep MPJE Online Law Review course, available at www.rxprep.com

Pamela Tu, PharmD

Karen Shapiro, PharmD, BCPS

with Matthew Seamon, PharmD, JD

RXPREP, INC.

PRIMARY SOURCES

Food and Drug Administration, at www.fda.gov

National Association of Boards of Pharmacy, at www.nabp.net

DEA's Pharmacist's Manual, at www.deadiversion.usdoj.gov/pubs/manuals/pharm2/

U.S. Pharmacopeial Chapters, at www.usp.org

VERSION 1.3

Cover Design by CreativeShoeBox.com

Book Design by MidnightBookFactory.com

Please Review:

On behalf of RxPrep, welcome to our MPJE® exam review. This booklet is to be used with RxPrep's online MPJE® course. The course includes videos that explain and summarize each topic. The videos correspond with the online test bank sections. You will be able to test your knowledge retention with the test banks.

If you are not sure how to master the details required, you may wish to follow the instructions on "how to do well" when testing that are located under the Announcement section on your student dashboard page. You will reach the student dashboard page when logged into your account on the RxPrep website through a computer.

Several of the tables in the text contain information that may have changed (such as requirements for intern hours or continuing education). Select tables are kept online and updated as needed. If you are aware of updates in your state, or have questions for the instructors, you are welcome to send an email to instructors@rxprep.com.

This course is based on the NABP exam bulletin of April 2016. If RxPrep has prepared updates based on revisions to the exam requirements or on the competency statements, the update/s will be posted online.

Announcements about updates are sent to the RxPrep mobile application on your hand-held device, and are posted to the Announcement section on the student dashboard page.

We wish you the best for your MPJE® preparation.

The RxPrep Team
www.rxprep.com

TABLE OF CONTENTS

[Handwritten notes at top of page:]

USP 795 Non-Sterile Comp.
USP 797 Sterile compounding
USP 800 Hazardous drugs (Chemo/Oncology/Hematology)

NIOSH - National Institute for Occupational Safety & Health
* maintains a list of hazardous drugs used in healthcare settings (updated every other year/even yrs)

Example:
* Methotrexate
* Hydroxy urea
* Megestrol
* Fluorouracil
* Tamoxifen

Introduction to the Multistate Pharmacy Jurisprudence Exam

INTRODUCTION TO THE STATE LAW EXAMS

Review the latest exam registration bulletin that is available for download on the National Association of Boards of Pharmacy (NABP) website.[1] The bulletin discusses the NAPLEX and MPJE, the registration process, scheduling the exam, testing and reporting results, the test design, and the specific topics that will be tested.

This course is based on the NABP bulletin issued April 2016. If RxPrep has prepared updates, these will be posted with your online course access, and can be printed out when logged into your account on the RxPrep website through a computer.

A few states and jurisdictions develop their own law exams and do not use the MPJE (Arkansas, California, Guam, Puerto Rico, and the Virgin Islands). Even in states that have their own exams, the federal law applies to all states and the requirements that are discussed in this course will apply. All states and jurisdictions require passing the NAPLEX, with the exception of Puerto Rico, where pharmacists can take either the NAPLEX or the Puerto Rico exam.

There is no distinction on the exam between federal law and state law. The state board will specify what they require on the state's version of the MPJE, which will be in addition to the federal law requirements. State boards cannot weaken any existing federal regulations, but they can make them more stringent, and may add requirements. Each state board selects the questions from the MPJE competency statements and can develop their own questions. The applicant is responsible for checking with the specific state board/s in which they are testing to make sure that the items the board requires are well known prior to testing. The state board of pharmacy website may list recommended study materials for the MPJE.

To find the state board in which you wish to become licensed, click on the state on the NABP's website.[2] It is helpful to complete your intern hours in the state in which you plan to become licensed in order to become familiar with the law as it applies in practice.

---

1 http://www.nabp.net/programs/examination/mpje (accessed 2015 Aug 4).
2 http://www.nabp.net/boards-of-pharmacy (accessed 2015 Aug 4).

NABP conducts an annual survey of many of the state-specific requirements, which is available on a compact disc (CD). The survey includes all 50 states, the District of Columbia, Guam and Puerto Rico. The CD provides a brief and easy way to review select legal requirements for each state and jurisdiction in which the applicant may wish to become licensed. The CD is provided to each pharmacy graduate of ACPE-certified schools. U.S. pharmacy school graduates should contact their school to obtain this CD if they have not received one; the Advanced Pharmacy Practice Experience (APPE) office staff may be aware of where the CDs are located.

All states participate in "reciprocity" where the NAPLEX scores obtained for one state can be transferred for use in another state. There can be time limits for reciprocity set by each state. The MPJE is specific to the law in an individual state, and a score received in one state will not be valid in any other. Candidates must take a separate MPJE for each state or jurisdiction in which they plan to become licensed.

The majority of the MPJE questions will come from the topics discussed in this course, and state-specific items are included as-needed. In this booklet, you will need to "fill-in" specific requirements where they vary state-to-state.

Mastering the test bank questions that come with this course completely (with an understanding of "why" the answer is correct) will help you achieve a good score. A method that works well on how to manage the preparation for pharmacy licensing exams is available under the "Announcement" section of the student dashboard page, which is visible when logged into your RxPrep account through a computer.

The MPJE (and the NAPLEX) are taken at Pearson VUE testing centers. The national board fee for the MPJE is $250, and the states have their own fees, which can include costs for fingerprinting and other types of documentation.

There are three competency areas tested on the exam:

■ Area I tests on legal aspects of pharmacy practice.

■ Area II tests on licensure, registration, certification, and operational requirements.

■ Area III tests regulations that affect pharmacies, prescribers, pharmacists, healthcare facilities, drug manufacturers, and distributors.

The MPJE is a 2.5-hour, 120 question, computer-adaptive examination. "Adaptive" means that the exam questions will adapt to the tester's ability level. Of the 120 questions, 100 questions count towards the grade. The other 20 questions are pretest questions and do not count. The board uses the pretest questions to determine if they are appropriate for use in future exams. These are dispersed throughout the test and there is no way to tell if a specific question will be counted. It is important to answer each question as best as possible.

The question types include multiple-choice, select all that apply (SATA), "K-type" (which include single or multiple correct responses, such as selecting options I, II and III) and ranking questions (the steps for a procedure are presented out of order, and the tester has to move them into the correct order). It is not possible to go back and change previously selected answer choices.

To receive an MPJE score, 107 exam questions must be completed. If more than 107 but less than 120 questions are answered, a penalty will be applied to the score. It is best to be well prepared and be able to complete the exam. A passing score is 75 points.

AGENCIES GOVERNING PHARMACY LAW

It is not possible to locate a law book issued by one federal agency that combines all federal requirements for the legal practice of pharmacy because there are different independent agencies involved in setting the requirements. In addition to federal requirements, the pharmacist will need to be in legal accordance with the statutes and regulations set by the state in which the pharmacy is licensed. A few examples of agencies that set the requirements for pharmacy practice include:

- Controlled substances are regulated by the Drug Enforcement Administration (DEA).
  The DEA enforces the Controlled Substances Act (CSA) and is involved with all aspects of controlled substances, from the theft of a bottle of OxyContin to monitoring international drug smuggling rings.

- Child-resistant drug packaging requirements are set by the Poison Prevention Packaging Act, which is under the U.S. Consumer Product Safety Commission.
  This act is an attempt to limit toxin exposure from various chemical compounds, including prescription and OTC drugs.

- Privacy requirements for protected health information are set by the Department of Health and Human Services, under the HIPAA regulations.

- Requirements for pseudoephedrine-containing products are set by the Control Methamphetamine Epidemic Act (CMEA).
  This act was included in an amendment to the U.S. Patriot Act, which passed Congress in October, 2001, and was extended in 2015.

- The state's Board of Pharmacy is directly involved with making sure the pharmacy is operating in accordance with federal and state legal requirements.
  The state board is not permitted to weaken federal requirements; they can either adopt them as-is, or strengthen them. For example, tramadol was scheduled as schedule IV in many states prior to the DEA scheduling the drug as schedule IV nationwide. Pharmacy and pharmacist-specific items (such as granting a license to practice in that state, setting continuing education requirements, permitting pharmacists to take scheduled work breaks, permitting off-site storage of certain pharmacy records and other such matters), are set by the state.

MPJE COMPETENCY STATEMENTS

MPJE Competency Statements

The MPJE Competency Statements provide a blueprint of the topics covered on the examination. They offer important information about the knowledge, judgment, and skills you are expected to demonstrate while taking the MPJE. A strong understanding of the Competency Statements will aid you in your preparation to take the examination.

Your formal education, training, practical experience, and self-study prepare you for the MPJE. The MPJE has been designed to assess how well you apply your knowledge, skills, and abilities to evaluate situations involving the applicable federal and state laws and regulations that govern the practice of pharmacy in the state in which you are seeking licensure. Additional information may also be obtained from the state board of pharmacy where you are seeking licensure.

Note: No distinction is made in the examination between federal and state jurisprudence questions. You are required to answer each question in terms of the prevailing laws of the state in which you are seeking licensure.

Area 1 Pharmacy Practice (Approximately 83% of Test)

1.1   *Legal responsibilities of the pharmacist and other pharmacy personnel*

    1.1.1   Unique legal responsibilities of the pharmacist-in-charge (or equivalent), pharmacists, interns, and pharmacy owners
- Responsibilities for inventory, loss and/or theft of prescription drugs, the destruction/disposal of prescription drugs and the precedence of Local, State, or Federal requirements

1.1.2   *Qualifications, scope of duties, and conditions for practice relating to pharmacy technicians and all other non-pharmacist personnel*
- Personnel ratios, duties, tasks, roles, and functions of non-pharmacist personnel

1.2   *Requirements for the acquisition and distribution of pharmaceutical products, including samples*

    1.2.1   Requirements and record keeping in relation to the ordering, acquiring, and maintenance of all pharmaceutical products and bulk drug substances/excipients
- Legitimate suppliers, pedigrees and the maintenance of acquisition records

1.2.2   *Requirements for distributing pharmaceutical products and preparations, including the content and maintenance of distribution records*
- Legal possession of pharmaceutical products (including drug samples), labeling, packaging, repackaging, compounding, and sales to practitioners

1.3   *Legal requirements that must be observed in the issuance of a prescription/drug order*

    1.3.1   Prescription/order requirements for pharmaceutical products and the limitations on their respective therapeutic uses
- Products, preparations, their uses and limitations applicable to all prescribed orders for both human and veterinary uses

    1.3.2   Scope of authority, scope of practice, and valid registration of all practitioners who are authorized under law to prescribe, dispense, or administer pharmaceutical products, including controlled substances
- Federal and State registrations, methadone programs, office-based opioid treatment programs, regulations related to retired or deceased prescribers, Internet prescribing, limits on jurisdictional prescribing

    1.3.3   Conditions under which the pharmacist participates in the administration of pharmaceutical products, or in the management of patients' drug therapy
- Prescriptive authority, collaborative practice, consulting, counseling, medication administration (including immunization, vaccines), ordering labs, medication therapy management, and disease state management

    1.3.4   Requirements for issuing a prescription/order
- Content and format for written, telephonic voice transmission, electronic facsimile, computer and Internet, during emergency conditions, and tamper-resistant prescription forms.

    1.3.5   Requirements for the issuance of controlled substance prescriptions/orders

---

- Content and format for written, telephonic voice transmission, electronic facsimile, computerized and Internet, during emergency conditions, conditions for changing a prescription, time limits for dispensing initial prescriptions/drug orders, and requirements for multiple Schedule II orders

1.3.6   Limits of a practitioner's authority to authorize refills of a pharmaceutical product, including controlled substances

1.4   *Procedures necessary to properly dispense a pharmaceutical product, including controlled substances, pursuant to a prescription/drug order*

1.4.1   Responsibilities for determining whether prescriptions/orders were issued for a legitimate medical purpose and within all applicable legal restrictions
- Corresponding responsibility, maximum quantities, restricted distribution systems, red flags/automated alerts, controlled substances, valid patient / prescriber relationship, and due diligence to ensure validity of the order

1.4.2   Requirements for the transfer of existing prescription/order information from one pharmacist to another

1.4.3   Conditions under which a prescription/order may be filled or refilled
- Emergency fills or refills, partial dispensing of a controlled substance, disaster or emergency protocol, patient identification, requirement for death with dignity, medical marijuana, and conscience /moral circumstances

1.4.4   Conditions under which prospective drug use review is conducted prior to dispensing
- Patient-specific therapy and requirements for patient-specific documentation

1.4.5   Conditions under which product selection is permitted or mandated
- Consent of the patient and/or prescriber, passing-on of cost savings, and appropriate documentation

1.4.6   Requirements for the labeling of pharmaceutical products and preparations dispensed pursuant to a prescription/order
- Generic and therapeutic equivalency, formulary use, auxiliary labels, patient package inserts, FDA medication guides, and written drug information

1.4.7   Packaging requirements of pharmaceutical products, preparations, and devices to be dispensed pursuant to a prescription/order
- Child-resistant and customized patient medication packaging

1.4.8   Conditions under which a pharmaceutical product, preparation, or device may not be dispensed
- Adulteration, misbranding, and dating

1.4.9   Requirements for compounding pharmaceutical products
- Environmental controls, release checks and testing, beyond use date (BUD), initial and ongoing training

1.4.10   Requirements for emergency kits
- Supplying, maintenance, access, security, and inventory

1.4.11   Conditions regarding the return and/or reuse of pharmaceutical products, preparations, bulk drug substances/excipients, and devices
- Charitable programs, cancer or other repository programs, previously dispensed, and from ""will call"" areas of pharmacies

1.4.12   Procedures and requirements for systems or processes whereby a non-pharmacist may obtain pharmaceutical products, preparations, bulk drug substances/excipients, and devices
- Pyxis (vending), after hour's access, telepharmacies, and secure automated patient drug retrieval centers

1.4.13   Procedures and requirements for establishing and operating central processing and central fill pharmacies
- Remote order verification

1.4.14   Requirements for reporting to PMP, accessing information in a PMP and the maintenance of security and confidentiality of information accessed in PMPs

1.4.15   Requirements when informed consent must be obtained from the patient and/or a duty to warn must be executed
- Collaborative practice and investigational drug therapy

1.5   *Conditions for making an offer to counsel or counseling appropriate patients, including the requirements for documentation*

1.5.1   Requirements to counsel or to make an offer to counsel

1.5.2   Required documentation necessary for counseling

1.6 *Requirements for the distribution and/or dispensing of non-prescription pharmaceutical products, including controlled substances*

    1.6.1 Requirements for the labeling of non-prescription pharmaceutical products and devices

    1.6.2 Requirements for the packaging and repackaging of non-prescription pharmaceutical products and devices

    1.6.3 Requirements for the distribution and/or dispensing of poisons, restricted, non-prescription pharmaceutical products, and other restricted materials or devices
- Pseudoephedrine, dextromethorphan, emergency contraception, and behind the counter products as appropriate

1.7 *Procedures for keeping records of information related to pharmacy practice, pharmaceutical products and patients, including requirements for protecting patient confidentiality*

    1.7.1 Requirements pertaining to controlled substance inventories

    1.7.2 Content, maintenance, storage, and reporting requirements for records required in the operation of a pharmacy
- Prescription filing systems, computer systems and backups, and prescription monitoring programs

    1.7.3 Requirements for protecting patient confidentiality and confidential health records
- HIPAA requirements and conditions for access and use of information

1.8 *Requirements for handling hazardous materials such as described in USP <800>*

    1.8.1 Requirements for appropriate disposal of hazardous materials

    1.8.2 Requirements for training regarding hazardous materials
- Reverse distributors, quarantine procedures, comprehensive safety programs, Material Safety Data Sheets

    1.8.3 Environmental controls addressing the proper storage, handling, and disposal of hazardous materials
- Ventilation controls, personal protective equipment, work practices, and reporting

    1.8.4 Methods for the compounding, dispensing and administration of hazardous materials
- All hazardous materials including sterile and non-sterile compounding

Area 2 – Licensure, Registration, Certification, and Operational Requirements (15%)

2.1 *Qualifications, application procedure, necessary examinations, and internship for licensure, registration, or certification of individuals engaged in the storage, distribution, and/or dispensing of pharmaceutical products (prescription and non-prescription)*

    2.1.1 Requirements for special or restricted licenses, registration, authorization, or certificates
- Pharmacists, pharmacist preceptors, pharmacy interns, pharmacy technicians, controlled substance registrants, and under specialty pharmacist licenses (Nuclear, Consultant etc.)

    2.1.2 Standards of practice related to the practice of pharmacy
- Quality assurance programs (including peer review), changing dosage forms, therapeutic substitution, error reporting, public health reporting requirements (such as notification of potential terrorist event, physical abuse, and treatment for tuberculosis), and issues of conscience and maintaining competency

    2.1.3 Requirements for classifications and processes of disciplinary actions that may be taken against a registered, licensed, certified, or permitted individual

    2.1.4 Requirements for reporting to, and participating in, programs addressing the inability of an individual licensed, registered, or certified by the Board to engage in the practice of pharmacy with reasonable skill and safety
- Impairment caused by the use of alcohol, drugs, chemicals, or other materials, or mental, physical, or psychological conditions

2.2 *Requirements and application procedure for the registration, licensure, certification, or permitting of a practice setting or business entity*

    2.2.1 Requirements for registration, license, certification, or permitting of a practice setting
- In-state pharmacies, out-of-state pharmacies, specialty pharmacies, controlled substance registrants, wholesalers, distributors, manufacturers/repackagers, computer services providers, and internet pharmacies

    2.2.2 Requirements for an inspection of a licensed, registered, certified, or permitted practice setting

    2.2.3 Requirements for the renewal or reinstatement of a license, registration, certificate, or permit of a practice setting

2.2.4 Classifications and processes of disciplinary actions that may be taken against a registered, licensed, certified, or permitted practice setting

2.3 *Operational requirements for a registered, licensed, certified, or permitted practice setting*

2.3.1 Requirements for the operation of a pharmacy or practice setting that is not directly related to the dispensing of pharmaceutical products
- Issues related to space, equipment, advertising and signage, security (including temporary absences of the pharmacist), policies and procedures, libraries and references (including veterinary), and the display of licenses

2.3.2 Requirements for the possession, storage, and handling of pharmaceutical products, preparations, bulk drug substances/excipients, and devices, including controlled substances
- Investigational new drugs, repackaged or resold drugs, sample pharmaceuticals, recalls, and outdated pharmaceutical products

2.3.3 Requirements for delivery of pharmaceutical products, preparations, bulk drug substances/excipients, and devices, including controlled substances
- Issues related to identification of the person accepting delivery of a drug, use of the mail, contract delivery, use of couriers, use of pharmacy employees, use of kiosks, secure mail boxes, script centers, use of vacuum tubes, and use of drive-up windows

Area 3 – General Regulatory Processes (2%)

3.1 *Application of regulations*

3.1.1 Laws and rules that regulate or affect the manufacture, storage, distribution, and dispensing of pharmaceutical products, preparations, bulk drug substances/excipients, and devices, (prescription and non-prescription), including controlled substances
- Food, Drug, and Cosmetic Act(s) and Regulations, the Controlled Substances Act(s) and Regulations, OBRA 90's Title IV Requirements, Practice Acts and Rules, other statutes and regulations, including but not limited to, dispensing of methadone, child-resistant packaging, tamper resistant packaging, drug paraphernalia, drug samples, pharmacist responsibilities in Medicare-certified skilled-nursing facilities, NDC numbers, and schedules of controlled substances

MPJE Sample Questions

The following are examples of question types that examinees may encounter when taking the MPJE. These questions are presented as examples to familiarize examinees with their formats and are not intended to represent content areas on the MPJE. Every examinee is presented with the opportunity to take a tutorial at the testing center prior to initiating the MPJE. The tutorial instructs examinees on how to respond to all of the types of questions that could be presented on the examination. NABP strongly encourages each examinee to take the tutorial in order to become familiar with how to submit responses in the computer-based examination.

Multiple-Choice Question Format

How many total continuing pharmacy education hours are required to be completed upon the second renewal of a pharmacist's license in this jurisdiction?

A. 15

B. 20

C. 25

D. 30

E. 40

Multiple-Response Question Format

Which of the following medications are classified as Schedule II controlled substances in this jurisdiction? (Select **ALL** that apply.)

A. Strattera

B. Lisdexamfetamine

C. Meprobamate

D. Amphetamine

E. Dexmethylphenidate

Ordered-Response Question Format

Place the following in the order in which they would expire according to federal regulations, starting with the earliest.

(**ALL** options must be used.)

Left-click the mouse to highlight, drag, and order the answer options.

Unordered Options	Ordered Response
A partially filled methylphenidate prescription for a patient not in a long-term care facility	
A phoned-in, emergency oxycodone prescription	
A written bupropion prescription	
An electronic alprazolam prescription	
A partially filled morphine prescription for a patient in a long-term care facility	

The State Boards of Pharmacy

Each state and jurisdiction has a board of pharmacy (or a similar body) whose primary purpose is to protect the public health. The board is responsible for granting and revoking professional licenses for pharmacists and other licensed personnel in the state who practice in a pharmacy. The board sets the requirements for the intern hours required to sit for licensure, and the continuing pharmacy education (CPE) hours and requirements that must be maintained by licensed pharmacists. The board will meet on a scheduled basis to review the rules and regulations set by the state and amend these, or add new requirements, when it is necessary.

The board will consist of some variation of public and professional members who serve at designated terms of length, and will be under the directorship of an executive who is assisted by various staff members. The board will oversee pharmacy inspectors who inspect the individual pharmacies to ensure compliance with federal and state laws and regulations.

How many public members (non-pharmacists) serve on the board of pharmacy in your state? _____

How many pharmacist members serve on the board of pharmacy in your state?_____

What is the term of service (length of years)?_____

Pharmacy Laws and Regulations

Laws are enacted through a federal or state legislative process. Regulations, or rules, provide specific details to help implement the law, and are issued by state regulatory agencies. In pharmacy, most of the rules and regulations are enacted through the state boards of pharmacy. This section discusses the history and practical use of drug laws and regulations in the United States, beginning with the FDA and the U.S. drug approval process.

THE FOOD AND DRUG ADMINISTRATION

The Food and Drug Administration (FDA), in its own words, is "responsible for protecting the public health by assuring the safety, efficacy and security of human and veterinary drugs, biological products, medical devices, our nation's food supply, cosmetics, and products that emit radiation".[4] The FDA splits up the responsibilities among six centers. The largest center is the one that is most important for pharmacy—the Center for Drug Evaluation and Research (CDER). CDER reviews the drug data provided through the FDA's drug approval process in order to make sure that the drugs marketed in the U.S. are safe and effective.

CBER - Biological Evaluation & research; CFNF food & nutrition safety

The Drug Approval Process

The drug approval process begins with pre-clinical testing on animals, which are generally rodents. This is called "pre-clinical" research because it comes before the "clinical" research that uses human subjects. If the pre-clinical animal research appears to indicate a relatively safe drug with a potential therapeutic use, the manufacturer will file an investigational new drug (IND) application with the FDA. The IND approval represents the FDA's permission to begin the Phase I clinical studies in human subjects. All phases of the clinical trial will involve

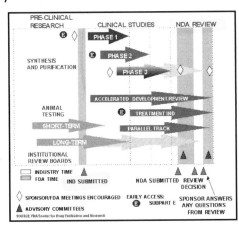

Timeline of the FDA's drug approval process.

4   http://www.fda.gov/AboutFDA/WhatWeDo/ (accessed 2015 Jun 02).

the drug's safety. If a drug is found to be particularly unsafe at any phase, the FDA may halt the clinical trial entirely.

Pre-clinical — Animals (multiple types; dogs, rabbits)

PHASE	SUBJECTS	PURPOSE
Phase I	Healthy subjects ~ 20 – 80	Safety, adverse effects *healthy male volunteers.* Pharmacokinetics and pharmacodynamics
Phase II *2-5 yrs.*	Patients ~ 35 - 100 *200*	Safety and efficacy *★* (Dosing range studied) *ex 20 mg no problem; vs 2g small problem*
Phase III	Patients ~ 300 – 3,000 *2000*	Efficacy for treating the condition compared to a placebo or gold-standard treatment *If completed successfully the manufacturer files an NDA or BLA*
Phase IV	Patients	Post-marketing surveillance

+ Determine new indications

The purpose of phase I, in addition to safety, is to assess adverse effects, including common side effects, and the drug's pharmacokinetics and pharmacodynamics, including absorption, distribution, metabolism and excretion.

Phase II studies focus on the safety and efficacy. Efficacy means that the drug provides benefit for the given purpose. The subjects in the phase II trials have the indicated condition; for example, if a new agent has been developed to remove plaque in patients with coronary artery disease, the subjects in phase II will have coronary artery disease. This is when dose-ranging is analyzed. The trial will be designed to determine the optimum dose (or dose range) for the given condition.

Phase III studies focus on the safety and efficacy at the given dose/s and schedule. Phase III is the final step before submitting to the FDA a new drug application (NDA) or if a biologic, a biologics license application (BLA).

The NDA or BLA is the complete package of information on the drug and will include all the collected animal data, human data, the pharmacokinetic and pharmacodynamic analysis, including drug interaction studies, and a complete review of the manufacturing process. This material will be evaluated by the FDA through CDER. In accordance with the Prescription Drug User Fee Act (PDUFA), which is discussed further, CDER is expected to review 90% of applications for standard drugs within 10 months of receiving the application, and within 6 months for priority drugs.

Phase IV studies, commonly referred to as post-marketing surveillance studies, may be conducted after the drug is approved and released for use. The FDA might request a post-marketing phase IV study to examine the risks and benefits of the new drug in a different population or to conduct special monitoring in a high-risk population that showed concern during the clinical testing. Alternatively, a phase IV study might be initiated by the manufacturer to assess such issues as the long-term effects of drug exposure.

Prescribing Information Approval

When a drug is approved, the prescribing information (the "package insert") is approved concurrently. The top section contains the prescribing information "Highlights", followed by the detailed information. The labeling must include these categories:

- Indications and Usage
- Dosage and Administration
- Dosage Forms and Strengths
- Boxed Warnings, if present
- Contraindications
- Warnings and Precautions
- Adverse Reactions
- Drug Interactions

- Use in Specific Populations (including pregnancy, nursing, pediatrics and geriatrics)
- Description
- Clinical Pharmacology
- Clinical Studies
- References
- How Supplied/Storage and Handling
- Patient Counseling Information

HIGHLIGHTS OF PRESCRIBING INFORMATION

These highlights do not include all the information needed to use EVISTA safely and effectively. See full prescribing information for EVISTA.

EVISTA (raloxifene hydrochloride) Tablet for Oral Use

Initial U.S. Approval: 1997

WARNING: INCREASED RISK OF VENOUS THROMBOEMBOLISM AND DEATH FROM STROKE

See full prescribing information for complete boxed warning.

- **Increased risk of deep vein thrombosis and pulmonary embolism have been reported with EVISTA (5.1). Women with active or past history of venous thromboembolism should not take EVISTA (4.1).**
- **Increased risk of death due to stroke occurred in a trial in postmenopausal women with documented coronary heart disease or at increased risk for major coronary events. Consider risk-benefit balance in women at risk for stroke (5.2, 14.5).**

------------------------RECENT MAJOR CHANGES------------------------

None.

------------------------INDICATIONS AND USAGE------------------------

EVISTA® is an estrogen agonist/antagonist indicated for:
- Treatment and prevention of osteoporosis in postmenopausal women. (1.1)
- Reduction in risk of invasive breast cancer in postmenopausal women with osteoporosis. (1.2)
- Reduction in risk of invasive breast cancer in postmenopausal women at high risk for invasive breast cancer. (1.3)

Important Limitations: EVISTA is not indicated for the treatment of invasive breast cancer, reduction of the risk of recurrence of breast cancer, or reduction of risk of noninvasive breast cancer. (1.3)

------------------------DOSAGE AND ADMINISTRATION------------------------

60 mg tablet orally once daily. (2.1)

------------------------DOSAGE FORMS AND STRENGTHS------------------------

Tablets (not scored): 60 mg (3)

------------------------CONTRAINDICATIONS------------------------

- Active or past history of venous thromboembolism, including deep vein thrombosis, pulmonary embolism, and retinal vein thrombosis. (4.1)
- Pregnancy, women who may become pregnant, and nursing mothers. (4.2, 8.1, 8.3)

------------------------WARNINGS AND PRECAUTIONS------------------------

- *Venous Thromboembolism*: Increased risk of deep vein thrombosis, pulmonary embolism, and retinal vein thrombosis. Discontinue use 72 hours prior to and during prolonged immobilization. (5.1, 6.1)
- *Death Due to Stroke*: Increased risk of death due to stroke occurred in a trial in postmenopausal women with documented coronary heart disease or at increased risk for major coronary events. No increased risk of stroke was seen in this trial. Consider risk-benefit balance in women at risk for stroke. (5.2, 14.5)
- *Cardiovascular Disease*: EVISTA should not be used for the primary or secondary prevention of cardiovascular disease. (5.3, 14.5)
- *Premenopausal Women*: Use is not recommended. (5.4)
- *Hepatic Impairment*: Use with caution. (5.5)
- *Concomitant Use with Systemic Estrogens*: Not recommended. (5.6)
- *Hypertriglyceridemia*: If previous treatment with estrogen resulted in hypertriglyceridemia, monitor serum triglycerides. (5.7)

------------------------ADVERSE REACTIONS------------------------

Adverse reactions (>2% and more common than with placebo) include: hot flashes, leg cramps, peripheral edema, flu syndrome, arthralgia, sweating. (6.1)

To report SUSPECTED ADVERSE REACTIONS, contact Eli Lilly and Company at 1-800-545-5979 or FDA at 1-800-FDA-1088 or www.fda.gov/medwatch

------------------------DRUG INTERACTIONS------------------------

- *Cholestyramine*: Use with EVISTA is not recommended. Reduces the absorption and enterohepatic cycling of raloxifene. (7.1, 12.3)
- *Warfarin*: Monitor prothrombin time when starting or stopping EVISTA. (7.2, 12.3)
- *Highly Protein-Bound Drugs*: Use with EVISTA with caution. Highly protein-bound drugs include diazepam, diazoxide, and lidocaine. EVISTA is more than 95% bound to plasma proteins. (7.3, 12.3)

------------------------USE IN SPECIFIC POPULATIONS------------------------

- Pediatric Use: Safety and effectiveness not established. (8.4)

See 17 for PATIENT COUNSELING INFORMATION and Medication Guide

Revised: 01/2011

The Highlights of the Prescribing Information for Evista. The complete labeling information, with all the information required, will be included on the following pages of the package insert.

FDA Review Periods and User Fees

Under the 1992 Prescription Drug User Fee Act (PDUFA), the FDA was given authority to collect fees from the "user" (the drug's manufacturer) in order for the FDA to review the new drug applications and supplements. The FDA uses these funds to hire reviewers to help expedite the review process. The fees are ~$2 million dollars for a review that contains clinical data.

The act gave the FDA conditions under which these funds could be collected: 90% of priority drugs will be reviewed within 6 months, and 90% of standard drugs will be reviewed within 10 months. The average cost to bring a drug into market is ~$500 million.

The Over-the-Counter Drug Approval Process

Over-the-counter (OTC) drugs are approved either with the same NDA process used for prescription drugs, or can be approved through the simpler OTC drug monograph process. The OTC monograph approval process has three steps, which the FDA calls a "three-phase public rulemaking process". Each phase requires a publication in the *Federal Register*, the federal government's daily 'newspaper', which is used to keep the public informed. The final version is the drug monograph. *NDA process*

In the first phase of the OTC monograph approval process, the FDA forms advisory review panels to review the active ingredients and determine whether they are "generally recognized as safe and effective" for use in self-treatment. The panels recommend appropriate labeling, including therapeutic indications, dosage instructions, and warnings about side effects and how to prevent misuse. The conclusions are published in the *Federal Register* in the form of an advanced notice of proposed rulemaking (ANPR). After publication of the ANPR, a period of time is given for any interested parties to submit comments or data in response to the proposal.

The second phase is the agency's review of active ingredients in each class of drugs, the public comments, and any new data that has become available. The FDA publishes its conclusions in the *Federal Register* in the form of a tentative final monograph (TFM). After publication of the TFM, a period of time is allotted for interested parties to submit comments or data in response to the monograph.

The publication of the final OTC drug monograph is the third and final phase of the OTC monograph approval process. The monograph will establish the conditions under which the OTC drug has been recognized as safe and effective. If a drug cannot comply with the drug monograph requirements, an IND and subsequent NDA review process will be required for the OTC drug to be approved, and released to the market. OTC drugs are discussed in a separate section.

RASE - recognized as safe & effective
(ex. coffeine in specific doses as a stimulant)

Generic Drug Approval and the Abbreviated New Drug Application

Generic drug approval requires an Abbreviated New Drug Application (ANDA), which was approved as part of the Hatch-Waxman Act. The ANDA process requires a review of the generic product's chemistry, the manufacturing controls, and the labeling. The review is abbreviated because it does not require pre-clinical animal studies and clinical studies with human subjects. The bioavailability data required with an NDA is replaced with a simpler bioequivalency analysis.

FDA Adverse Event Reporting System and MedWatch

All drugs cause some adverse events, which should be reported to the FDA's MedWatch program. The name implies the purpose of the program: MedWatch is designed to "watch" the medication use in the public and find the adverse events that were not found in the clinical trials. The "eyes" of MedWatch are healthcare professionals, including pharmacists. Reporting and responding to adverse events is part of the professional responsibility of a pharmacist. Patients can report to MedWatch directly. Healthcare professionals and patients can also report adverse events to the drug manufacturer, who is required to send the collected reports at quarterly intervals for the first 3 years after drug approval, including a special report for any serious and unexpected events. This is considered part of the phase IV post-marketing surveillance.

Even the most well-designed phase III studies cannot possibly uncover every problem that could become apparent once a product is used in the real world. This is due to a variety of reasons, including an adverse event with a rare incidence (which may not have appeared in the trial subjects), adverse reactions that affect patients who were excluded from the trials, effects from long-term drug exposure that were not observed within the duration of the clinical trials, and a lack of rigorous lab monitoring. If the FDA gathers enough adverse reaction reports linked to the drug, the package labeling will be amended to incorporate the concern. If the adverse reactions are serious enough, the FDA may mandate a risk evaluation and mitigation strategy (REMS) or have the drug removed from the market.

Unapproved Drugs Remain on the Market

There are drugs on the market that have never been through a formal FDA review process. Since 1938 and the passage of the Food, Drug and Cosmetic Act, there have been drugs in use (some of which remain in use) that never went through the formal drug approval process. Initially, these drugs were "grandfathered" into the law, which means that the rule did not apply because the drugs were commercially available prior to the rule's enactment. Over time, the FDA has been bringing these drugs into the approval process. For example, levothyroxine is a very old drug with a long history of product inconsistency. The FDA required all levothyroxine products to submit an NDA by August 2001, and all levothyroxine products have since gone through the FDA approval process or are off the market and no longer available. Other drugs have gone through the approval process, and were subsequently withdrawn due to toxicity concerns. Others remain unapproved. An unapproved drug will have an NDC number but will not be listed in the FDA's *Approved Drug Products with Therapeutic Equivalence Evaluations*, commonly known as the *Orange Book*.

The drug approval process described here did not always exist; it is a sad fact that awful misadventures with drugs have fostered the development of a safer process for bringing drugs into the U.S. market.

Direct-to-Consumer Advertising for Prescription Drugs

Prescription drug advertising is regulated primarily by the FDA. OTC drug advertising is regulated primarily by the Consumer Product Safety Commission, which is under the Federal Trade Commission (FTC).

In previous years, drug marketing was targeted primarily towards healthcare professionals. Now, manufacturers spend billions of dollars each year on direct-to-consumer (DTC) advertising, which is the promotion of drugs aimed directly at the patient, through television commercials and magazine advertisements. This is a good investment for the company's bottom line (i.e., profitability) but perhaps not as great a benefit for the patient, who may be persuaded to request a treatment based on advertisements that may not be the best option for their condition. DTC advertising is not federally legislated and FDA pre-approval is not required. The FDA requires that the advertisement copy be submitted for review at the same time as the advertisement is being released to the public. The FDA will get involved if there is a lack of accurate information about the drug and if the fair balance requirement has not been met. "Fair balance" means that the positive information about the drug must be balanced with the negative information. The side effect and safety concerns must be presented in a manner designed to have as similar an impact on the viewer as the drug's benefit for treating the stated condition.

The FDA's minimum requirements for what an advertisement must contain:

■ At least one approved use

■ The generic name

■ A brief summary or major statement or "adequate provision" of the drug's risks

Major statements or "adequate provisions" are required for broadcast ads, which are the primary form of advertising (TV, radio, and automated calls). A major statement, for example, is when a voice on the radio or television ad presents the drug's most important risks (very quickly)! This is supposed to be done in a clear and neutral voice. An adequate provision is a way for the audience to find the drug's important safety information, such as providing a toll-free number to obtain this information, or listing the prescribing information on a separate page in a magazine ad. If the ad is found to violate the law, the FDA will get involved to have the ad pulled. Violations typically include making unsupportable claims, leaving out risk information, failing to include an adequate provision, misrepresenting study data, overstating the benefits, or promoting use in patient groups that have not been studied. Any false or misleading statements in the advertisement could be considered misbranding.

Drug Recalls

Drug recalls are made for a variety of reasons, such as contamination with particles of glass or some type of toxin, variability of drug concentration, incomplete product labeling and stability concerns.

Recalls involve a drug that poses a danger; thus, classifying the recall properly and taking an action commensurate with the risk is required. Recalls are an expected occurrence in pharmacy practice.

Market Withdrawal

Manufacturers may withdraw a drug from the market for many reasons, which can be due to decreased market demand. The drug is not making enough money or extensive monitoring is required, which may prove to be too costly.

Counterfeit Drugs

Counterfeit drugs are fake, illegal drugs. The active ingredient may not be present, or may be in a lesser amount than stated, or another drug could be used as a substitute. Excipients may be harmful. These are produced by unethical persons who do not typically employ Current Good Manufacturing Practices (CGMPs). Counterfeit drugs have a higher likelihood of contamination and other quality concerns than what would be expected with FDA-regulated drugs.

The FDA is responsible for investigating counterfeit drug incidents. This involves illegal behavior and thus the investigation will be in cooperation with federal and state law enforcement.

The most newsworthy drugs with recent counterfeit versions include some of the erectile dysfunction drugs, the cancer drug *Avastin*, the stimulant *Adderall* and the emergency contraception product *Plan B One-Step*. Counterfeit versions can be identified by differences on the product labeling. For example, a counterfeit *Cialis* bottle did not include an NDC number, did not have the tablet strength in a colored box, had different patterns and colors, had misspellings in the name (*Cialis* is a product of: Eli Lilly Australia PTY Limited) and the production was in a different country. Most fake erectile dysfunction drugs contain some trace of the active pharmaceutical ingredient (API), which indicates that the theft involved a hole in the supply chain. On any given day, consumers can go online and find online pharmacies (discussed further) and order some of the common pain drugs, topical retinoids, stimulants, etc. It is risky to use these products. They could be lead-contaminated, or worse. This is not the same as ordering reputable products from a legitimate online pharmacy (described further).

SHERMAN ANTITRUST ACT OF 1890

The Sherman Antitrust Act attempted to outlaw monopolies that blocked competition by nefarious methods, such as price-fixing, deceptive marketing practices, and excluding competition from markets. This was a start in making more products available, including drug products, but did not address the issue of drug safety.

Prior to 1906, corruption and fraud were common and drug safety risks were found through trial and misadventure among the public. Some products in common use were safe, and others were not. This changed with the groundbreaking Pure Food and Drug Act of 1906.

PURE FOOD AND DRUG ACT OF 1906 (THE WILEY ACT)

The Pure Food and Drug Act was the first legislation in the U.S. that offered protection to consumers from drug misuse. Pressure on President Roosevelt to improve the safety of food and drugs had been building for years but got a final boost with the release of *The Jungle* by Upton Sinclair, which exposed the horrific conditions in the meat-packing industry. On June 30, 1906, President Roosevelt signed the Pure Food and Drug Act, otherwise known as the Wiley Act, which established both a meat inspection law and a comprehensive food and drug law.

The basis of the law involving drugs was to mandate accurate product labeling and to require that the ingredients used in drugs met the standards of strength, quality, and purity in the *United States Pharmacopoeia* (USP) and the *National Formulary (NF)*. The law required that the food or drug label could not be false or misleading, and the presence and amount of eleven dangerous ingredients, including alcohol, heroin, and cocaine, had to be listed.

The law required that no adulterated or misbranded drugs could be sent through interstate commerce. Adulteration means the drug itself is bad (drug quality is not up to standard) and misbranding means the label is inaccurate.

FOOD, DRUG AND COSMETIC ACT OF 1938

Diethylene glycol, used as a solvent in an oral preparation, resulted in fatalities.

In 1937, diethylene glycol was used as a solvent for an elixir preparation of sulfanilamide, an older sulfonamide antibiotic. This resulted in 107 deaths, most of which were children. The solvent in the untested product was a chemical analogue of antifreeze. The public outcry led to requirements for drugs to demonstrate safety prior to release. Congress enacted the Food, Drug, and Cosmetic Act (FDCA) in 1938, marking the birth of the modern FDA. The new act required that the manufacturer (not the FDA) prove the safety of a drug before it could be marketed. It authorized the FDA to conduct manufacturer and distributor inspections, and established penalties for using misleading labeling. From this point forward, the product claims must be accurate, and all ingredients must be listed on the label so that the public is aware of what they are ingesting. The amendments to the FDCA described on the following pages addressed deficiencies in the original act.

The definitions for food, drugs, dietary supplements and devices were defined by the FDCA for use in humans and other animals. Cosmetics were defined for human use only.

TERM	DEFINITION
Food	Items used for food or drink, the components in the food or drink, and chewing gum.
Drugs	Items recognized as drugs by the USP, NF and the official Homoeopathic Pharmacopoeia, and their supplements;
	Items used to diagnosis, cure, mitigate, treat or prevent disease;
	Items (other than food) intended to affect the structure or any function of the body.
Dietary Supplements	A product (other than tobacco) intended to supplement the diet that bears or contains one or more of the following ingredients: a vitamin, mineral, herb or other botanical, or amino acid, and their concentrates and extracts. These can be in combination;
	A dietary substance meant to supplement the diet by increasing the dietary intake and which is not used as the conventional food or as the sole item of a meal or the diet.
Devices	An instrument, apparatus, implement, machine, contrivance, implant, in vitro reagent, or similar that is recognized by USP;
	An item intended to be used in the diagnosis of disease or other conditions, or in the cure, mitigation, treatment, or prevention of disease;
	An item intended to affect the structure or any function of the body, and which does not achieve its primary intended purposes through chemical action and which is not dependent upon being metabolized.
Cosmetics	Items that are intended to be rubbed, poured, sprinkled, sprayed on, introduced into, or otherwise applied to the human body for cleansing, beautifying, promoting attractiveness, or altering the appearance, and the components of cosmetics, except soap (which is not a cosmetic).

The FDCA prohibited adulterated or misbranded drugs in interstate commerce. Adulteration involves the drug itself (the quality) and misbranding involves incorrect or missing information on the container or labeling. These are important concepts for the exam, since this involves giving unsafe drug.

Causes of Drug Adulteration: *"inside the drug" if the drug/product good.*

- It is filthy, putrid, or decomposed. *if decomposed*

- It has been prepared, packed, or stored under unsanitary conditions where it may have become contaminated with filth, or where it can become dangerous to a person's health. This includes a lack of adequate controls during the manufacturing process or a lack of tests that confirmed the quality and purity.

- It contains a drug recognized in official compendia, but its strength is different from official standards, or the purity or quality is lower than the official standards.

- It contains a drug not recognized in official compendia, but its strength is different from that listed on the label, or the purity or quality is lower than that listed on the label.

The official monographs of the United States Pharmacopoeia (USP) are used to make sure that the drug meets the requirements of the USP Chapter for the compound's identity, strength, quality and purity.[5]

if ant/spider got inside it's [adulteration]

Causes of Drug Misbranding: *outside of the bottle; involves labeling*

- If there is a lack of required information on the package and in the labeling (weight, count, warnings, use in specific groups, unsafe dosages, methods of use, treatment duration).

- If there is any false or misleading product information, such as imitating the properties of another drug, or promising false cures.

- If there is a lack of special precautions needed to prevent decomposition that must be specified on the packaging, such as "keep in original container" or "protect from humidity and light".

- If there is information that is illegible (cannot be read).

- If the packaging does not contain the proprietary (branded) or established common name (as recognized by USP or Homeopathic Pharmacopoeia).

- If the ingredients differ from the standard of strength, quality, or purity, as determined by the test laid in the USP monograph.

- If it does not contain the manufacturer and business location and packer or distributor.

- If there is improper packaging or improper or incomplete labeling of additives.

- If there is a deficiency in packaging according to the requirements of the Poison Prevention Packaging Act (described further).

5   USP and the National Formulary (NF) used to be separate organizations, and have since merged. The designation USP-NF is seen as a reference in some of the USP sources.

Ex. Gelatin has to be documented on the package insert (non-kosher)

Example #1

A packet labeled *Ortho Tri-Cyclen* contains ethinyl estradiol and norgestimate. Each blue tablet contains 0.25 mg norgestimate and 0.035 mg ethinyl estradiol. Each green tablet contains inert ingredients. The *Ortho Tri-Cyclen* is dispensed to a patient without a patient package insert.

A patient package insert must be dispensed with estrogen-containing products. This drug is misbranded.

Example #2

A bottle is labeled to contain levothyroxine 100 mcg per tablet. The bottle is found to contain particulate contaminants in the tablets.

The purity of the drug is compromised. The drug is adulterated.

PUBLIC HEALTH SERVICE ACT OF 1944

The Public Health Service (PHS) Act defined biological products (also called biologicals or biologics). Biologics come from organisms (including viruses, yeast, etc.), which normally can be infectious. Biologics are approved under a biologics license application (BLA), and not under an NDA as other drugs. The act required that biologics be approved for purity, potency and safety.

DURHAM-HUMPHREY AMENDMENT OF 1951 *Distinction btw RX & OTC.*

Hubert Humphrey   Carl Durham

The Durham-Humphrey Amendment was sponsored by two pharmacist-politicians, Congressman Carl Durham, a pharmacist from North Carolina, and Senator Hubert H. Humphrey, a pharmacist from South Dakota, who later became the 38th Vice President of the United States.

This was the first time that a clear distinction was made between OTC and prescription drugs. The amendment classified the three conditions that would make a drug available only by prescription:

■ Drugs that are habit-forming.

■ Drugs considered unsafe for use except under expert supervision due to toxicity concerns.

■ Drugs limited to prescription use only under a manufacturer's new drug application.

Another term used for prescription drugs are legend drugs. The term "legend" comes from the original legend required by the amendment to be placed on prescription drugs: "Caution: Federal law prohibits dispensing without a prescription." The requirement for this legend has since been simplified to "Rx Only" and is discussed further under the FDA Modernization Act of 1997.

OTC drugs were required to contain adequate directions for use in the "Drug Facts Label". The labeling must include safety in pregnancy and breast feeding, the calcium, sodium, magnesium and potassium content, and the product's U.S. contact information to report adverse events. Unit-dose labeling requirements were established, and are discussed further in the pharmacy practice section. The unit-dose container is common in the hospital setting as it improves efficiency and safety. The container has a barcode that can be scanned and matched to the patient's wristband, which enables the nurse to confirm that the correct medication will be administered to the correct patient. Additionally, the unit-dose container permits the drug to be placed in an automated dispensing system (ADS). The ADS has replaced the individual cassettes in many hospital settings. The cassettes were previously used to hold an individual patient's medications, and required considerable staff time to fill and replenish.

KEFAUVER-HARRIS AMENDMENT OF 1962 *safety & effectiveness*

In 1961, an Australian obstetrician reported an increase of severe malformations in children born to mothers using thalidomide, which was marketed as "the first safe sleeping pill" for use in pregnancy. It was also used for nausea during pregnancy. Although thalidomide was approved and was heavily marketed in Western Europe, the approval in the U.S. was blocked by a young pharmacologist, Dr. Frances Oldham Kelley, who had just started working at the FDA. She had concerns about the drug's safety and withstood heavy pressure to prevent release of the drug. This near catastrophe highlighted the need for more stringent laws regarding drug safety. Thalidomide is marketed in the U.S. today as *Thalomid* (along with related compounds) for cancer and complications of Hansen's disease, with a risk evaluation mitigation strategy to ensure safe use.

In 1962, Congress passed the Kefauver-Harris Amendment, which, for the first time, required that manufacturers prove to the FDA that a drug is both safe and effective for the claims made in the product's labeling. The safety and efficacy results should be achieved by conducting controlled investigations under the supervision of qualified researchers. It required manufacturers to maintain records of adverse events associated with drugs and report them to the FDA.

The Amendment created the NDA and the supplemental NDA (sNDA). The role of the institutional research board (IRB) was established for investigational new drugs. Drug studies in humans can begin only after an IND is reviewed by the FDA and a local IRB. The board is a panel of scientists and non-scientists in hospitals and research institutions that oversee the clinical research. The IRB is an important component of clinical trials; prior to this development, human subjects in clinical trials had little protection for their health and general welfare. Subjects had to give their informed consent, which means that a subject in a trial has a right to know what to expect, including all the risks and possible benefits, and must agree to participate with a signed consent form.

Advertising of drugs are regulated by the FDA (prescription drugs) and FTC (OTC drugs). Current Good Manufacturing Practices (CGMPs) are required for drug manufacturing, and included the following:

- Manufacturers must register with the FDA and must be inspected every 2 years.

- All drugs must come from a factory registered with the FDA or they are considered misbranded.

- If standards of strength, quality, or purity are lacking, the drug is considered adulterated.

CONTROLLED SUBSTANCES ACT OF 1970

The Controlled Substances Act (CSA) establishes the regulations that every registrant of the DEA, including pharmacies, must follow for all aspects of controlled substances, and is discussed in the controlled substances section.

✱ POISON PREVENTION AND PACKAGING ACT OF 1970 ✱ Exam Child-Resistant

Prior to implementation of the Poison Prevention and Packaging Act (PPPA), accidental poisoning was the top cause of injury in children less than 5 years old. There was literally no standard way to protect children from common dangerous substances, including drugs and dangerous household substances. The PPPA is enforced by the Consumer Product Safety Commission. It requires a number of household substances and drugs to be packaged in child-resistant (C-R) packaging. The packaging must be significantly difficult for children under 5 years of age to open within a reasonable time, and not difficult for normal adults to use properly. Drugs that require C-R packaging and those that do not is described in the pharmacy practice section.

*Pt can request blanket waiver (easy-cap). Pt. responsibility
*MD can request waiver for 1 specific drug.

DRUG LISTING ACT OF 1972

The Drug Listing Act of 1972 amended the FDCA to require drug establishments that are engaged in the manufacturing, preparation, propagation, compounding, or processing of a drug to register all of their drugs with the FDA. Each individual listed drug was required to have a unique national drug code (NDC) number.

The NDC is the product identifier that is present on all OTC and prescription drug packages and inserts. The code is 10 digits that are divided into 3 segments. The first segment is the labeler code and is assigned by the FDA. The second is the product code and the third is the package code. The second and third segments are assigned by the labeler.

The NDC is a "10-digit code with three segments:

- The first is the labeler code, assigned by the FDA, and is 4 or 5 digits.

- The second is the product code and identifies the strength, dosage and formulation and is 3 or 4 digits. (Mevacor/Lovastatin)

- The third is the package code and identifies the package size and type and is 1 or 2 digits. (100 tabs vs. 1000 tabs)

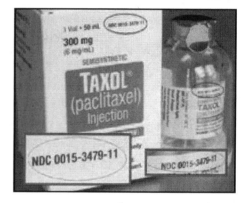

NDC Numbers

FEDERAL ANTI-TAMPERING ACT OF 1982

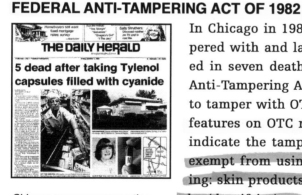

Chicago newspaper reporting on tainted Tylenol

In Chicago in 1982 bottles of OTC *Tylenol* tablets were tampered with and laced with potassium cyanide, which resulted in seven deaths. In response to this tragedy, the Federal Anti-Tampering Act was passed and made it a federal crime to tamper with OTC products, and required tamper-resistant features on OTC medications. The label of the package must indicate the tamper-resistant features. Certain products are exempt from using tamper-resistant features in the packaging: skin products, insulin, lozenges and tooth cleaning powder (dentifrice).

Ex: Tylenol, MTV, Pepcid

FEDERAL FALSE CLAIMS ACT OF 1982

The Federal False Claims Act made falsely billing Medicare and Medicaid a federal crime. It is used to prosecute companies that have contracted with one of these federal agencies and have overcharged for goods or services. If a person in or close to the company has information that the government is being falsely billed, the individual can report the overcharge/s and receive up to 25% of the recovered damages. The informants are referred to as "whistleblowers".

ORPHAN DRUG ACT OF 1983 *Has to go through regular approval process.*

In response to a major public campaign by people with rare diseases and their supporters, the Orphan Drug Act was approved in 1983. Prior to this act there was little motivation for pharmaceutical manufacturers to invest in drugs that would treat a relatively small number of people due to the limited potential return on the major investment required to get a drug to market. To get around this dilemma, the act authorized providing incentives to manufacturers to develop orphan drugs, including a tax credit for 50% of the clinical testing costs. Drugs are also given a 7-year period of exclusivity. Orphan drugs are developed under the FDA's Office of Orphan Products Development (OOPD). Drugs eligible for inclusion in this program include products that will treat diseases that affect less than 200,000 people in the United States, or for products with no reasonable expectation that the cost of research and development will be recovered by the sales revenue.

HATCH-WAXMAN ACT (*Drug* PRICE COMPETITION AND PATENT ACT) OF 1984

The FDCA did not specify any streamlined process for generic drug approval. Generic drugs required the same long and costly approval process as new drugs. Congress adopted the Hatch-Waxman Act (formerly referred to as the Drug Price Competition and Patent Term Restoration Act of 1984), to expedite and streamline both generic drug approvals and patent litigation involving generic drugs. Patent litigation (legal action) is used by pharmaceutical companies to prevent the release of generic competitors. The cost of litigation is typically much less than the profits obtained by blocking competing drugs. This is a boon to the company but a bane to the public. The purpose of the legislation was to increase the availability of generics and cut costs for the patient and the healthcare system. It shortened the approval process for generic drugs.

Provisions in the legislation have made it possible for generic drug companies to file one of two abbreviated applications for generic drug approval: the Abbreviated New Drug Application (ANDA), or the 505(b)(2) application, which is referred to as a paper NDA.

Under an ANDA, a generic drug company must provide study data to establish that the generic drug is effectively a duplicate of the

INACTIVE INGREDIENTS

Inactive ingredients are also called inert (which means chemically inactive) or excipients. Examples include fillers, extenders, diluents, wetting agents (surfactants), solvents, emulsifiers, preservatives, flavors and sweeteners, absorption enhancers, sustained-release matrices, and coloring agents.

The FDA defines an inactive ingredient as any component of a drug other than the active ingredient. Inactive ingredients do not affect the therapeutic action of the drug either by increasing or decreasing the effect.

Inactive ingredients are not always inert. For example, phenylalanine is a common sweetener, but can have a severe effect and must be avoided in patients with phenylketonuria, and the lipid emulsion that is used to deliver propofol can increase triglycerides in anyone. Inactive ingredients are listed in the CDER Ingredient Dictionary, which is part of the Orange Book. In addition to the name, each listing includes the unique ingredient identifier (UII), which is the ingredient's ID number, and the chemical abstracts service (CAS) number, which is provided by the American Chemical Society (ACS) and is used to search for detailed information on the component on the ACS website. The listing also includes the maximum amount that is permitted to be present in each dosage form.

Pharmacists check for inactive ingredients that can be harmful to certain patients, and there are many, including starch (with gluten-sensitivity), sulfites (with sulfite sensitivity) and soya lecithin (with peanut/soy allergy).

branded, NDA drug, which is called the Reference Listed Drug (RLD). This is based on bioequivalence cross-over studies between the generic and the RLD. The active ingredient, route, dosage and formulation must be the same as the RLD. The inactive ingredients (coloring, excipients, binders) can be different. The 505(b)(2) application, allows the sponsor to submit evidence of previously published reports of investigations of safety and effectiveness. Today, generic drugs, similar to branded drugs, are subject to user fees to help expedite the review process.

Established the Orange Book

PRESCRIPTION DRUG MARKETING ACT OF 1987

The Prescription Drug Marketing Act (PDMA) was enacted to reduce public health risks from adulterated, misbranded, counterfeit or expired drugs. The law prohibits reimportation: prescription drug products manufactured in the U.S. and subsequently exported to a foreign country cannot be reimported back into the U.S, except by the product's manufacturer. The sale of drug samples was prohibited. Drug samples are meant to be provided by the prescriber to the patient at no cost. The sale of drug coupons was prohibited. Drug coupons are either given to prescribers to provide to patients at no cost, or are given to consumers by the manufacturer in some type of product promotion, such as an advertisement. Patients cannot buy drugs in other countries and bring them into the U.S., except under either of these conditions:

- The quantity is for a ≤ 90-day supply, and is for the patient (cannot be resold).

- An effective treatment is not available in the U.S., the condition is serious, and the drug being imported has no unreasonable risk.

The patient may need to affirm the above in writing. Baggage is not supposed to be searched by law enforcement without a reasonable suspicion of the contents posing a risk to other travelers.

PDMA requires wholesalers to be state-licensed and meet uniform standards. It blocked hospitals from using drug re-sales as a normal part of business by placing strict limits on the percentage of drugs that hospital pharmacies can resell. A hospital that is large or is part of a chain, or a hospital that has government or other non-profit status, may be able to obtain drugs at a lower cost than other hospitals. In past years, it was a routine part of business at some hospitals to resell drugs that were obtained at a lower cost to other hospitals for a profit. Currently, selling drugs to another hospital (that is not part of the same hospital group) is only permitted in order to help the other hospital manage a drug shortage.

Prohibits re-importation
Prohibits the sale of drug samples
Prohibits the sale of drug coupons.

require counseling for Medicare & Medicaid pts. Have offer to counsel

OMNIBUS BUDGET RECONCILIATION ACT OF 1990

Concerns about improper medication use and inefficient use of federal dollars spent on healthcare led to the Omnibus Budget Reconciliation Act (OBRA). In the original OBRA legislation counseling was mandated for all Medicaid beneficiaries. Subsequently, both OBRA and the Centers for Medicare and Medicaid Services (CMS) required that the states establish counseling standards, which expanded counseling requirements for both Medicaid and non-Medicaid beneficiaries. As a result, all patients should receive counseling on their medications. Counseling requirements are reviewed in the pharmacy practice section.

DIETARY SUPPLEMENT HEALTH AND EDUCATION ACT OF 1994

The Dietary Supplement Health and Education Act (DSHEA) defined dietary supplements as food products. Prior to the signing of the DSHEA, dietary supplements were regulated in the same manner as drugs. Adulteration and misbranding remain prohibited, but otherwise dietary supplements are regulated quite differently. If the product includes a new dietary ingredient, the FDA will require a pre-market review for safety data. This is the only time a pre-market review is required. Otherwise, the company does not need to provide the FDA with safety and efficacy data and FDA approval is not needed prior to the release of the product and any related marketing material.

After the events of September 2011 manufacturers were required to register with the FDA prior to producing or selling dietary supplements under regulations in the Bioterrorism Act of 2002. This was enacted due to fears of bioterrorism.

ex. healthy heart product; will help with insomnia.

FDA EXPORT REFORM AND ENHANCEMENT ACT OF 1996

The Exportation Reform and Enhancement Act (EREA) was passed primarily in response to manufacturer's complaints that the FDA process to gain approval to export products under FDA jurisdiction was cumbersome and took excessive time. The manufacturers claimed that they were forced to move manufacturing facilities abroad (and the jobs that went with them) because the FDA did not authorize exportation in a timely manner. Actions that were permitted under the act included:

- FDA-approved drugs can be exported if they meet the other country's standards.

- Unapproved drugs can be exported only if they will be used in a clinical drug trial.

- The Active Pharmaceutical Ingredient (API) can be imported from a foreign manufacturer if being used for an FDA drug application, or for use in compounding. The API cannot be imported for manufacturing.

FDA MODERNIZATION ACT OF 1997

The FDA Modernization Act (FDAMA) brought the FDA into the 21st century. It required the establishment of a registry for clinical trials (available at clinicaltrials.gov), approved labeling changes for foods and drugs, enabled the manufacturer to discuss off-label drug use (when requested), and extended an amendment passed previously in 1992 (the Prescription Drug User Fee Act, or PDUFA) that permits the FDA to charge a manufacturer fees to expedite the drug review process.

FDAMA made a special exemption for compounding pharmacists to continue preparation of individualized drug products not otherwise available (as long as the requirements for manufacturing are not met).

Without accurate labeling a drug is misbranded. Previously, under the Durham-Humphrey Amendment, all prescription (i.e., legend) drugs required a label that included the statement "Caution: Federal law prohibits dispensing without a prescription." Under FDAMA the wording was simplified to "Rx only."

The FDAMA regulations permitting fast-track approval updated previous regulations that had been initiated in the 1980s. At this time, the human immunodeficiency virus (HIV) epidemic led to a public clamor for access to investigational drugs. Regulations were developed to accelerate approval for high-priority medications. The FDA now has four programs to help speed the development and review of new drugs that may alleviate or treat unmet medical needs in serious or life-threatening conditions: fast track designation, breakthrough therapy designation, accelerated approval, and priority review designation.

The FDA makes a primary judgment for faster approval based on whether the drug's benefit can justify the risk and defines a "surrogate endpoint" that is likely to predict a clinical benefit. If a patient is terminal and there is no treatment at present, it might be worth using a drug that might help but has not had the usual thorough review process. Patients with terminal illness are often desperate to get enrolled in an expedited trial. Many critics complain that the approval processes are still too cumbersome and slow; yet, the FDA does not wish to cause harm when it is attempting to provide benefit. In 2014, six of the 41 new drugs approved were under one of the accelerated approval programs.

THE DRUG ADDICTION TREATMENT ACT OF 2000

Opioid abuse and dependence is widespread in the United States. Prior to the Drug Addiction Treatment Act of 2000 (DATA 2000), the primary treatment was methadone, which was available only through a designated addiction clinic. These are not widely available and can stigmatize those seeking care. DATA 2000 permits practitioners to prescribe and dispense controlled substances in typical patient care settings, such as medical offices. This is described further under opioid treatment programs (OTP).

FDA AMENDMENTS ACT OF 2007

The FDA Amendments Act (FDAAA) gave new authority to the FDA to enhance drug safety. The Risk Evaluation and Mitigation Strategy (REMS) program was part of this legislation. A drug in which the FDA requires a REMS program will require more involvement from the manufacturer to ensure that the benefits of the drug or biologic outweigh the risks. These include various types of education and monitoring.

AFFORDABLE CARE ACT OF 2010

The Affordable Care Act (ACA), also known as "Obamacare", includes many provisions that are important to pharmacists. The American Pharmacists Association (APhA) has identified several areas that have a large impact on the profession of pharmacy:

- CMS Innovation Centers (CMSIC)

- Essential Health Benefits

- Medical Loss Ratio

- Integrated Care Models

- Transitional Care Models

- Improvements to Medicare Part D Medication Therapy Management (MTM)

If information on the ACA may be required, such as resolution of current legislative issues, these will be posted as an update to the MPJE course on the RxPrep website.

THE BIOLOGICS PRICE COMPETITION AND INNOVATION ACT OF 2010

Biologics are derived from living organisms (such as animals, microorganisms and yeast) and includes: vaccines, insulin, human growth hormone, erythropoietin, interferons, and others. Most of the specialty products are biologics. Conventional drugs (such as aspirin and lisinopril) are small and chemically-derived. Biologics are large and have a complex manufacturing process.

Only living organisms reproduce with this degree of complexity and there is some degree of variability even among the same biologic product. True "generics" for biologics are not possible according to the conventional definition, therefore the term "biosimilars" is used instead. The cost of a biosimilar approval is ~20-35% lower than the reference biologic, which is not the degree of cost savings expected with conventional drug generic approval (~75% cost savings), but considering the high cost of the original biologic, the savings can still be substantial.

The FDA was slow in developing a biosimilar approval process. In Europe, biosimilars have been used since 2003 and are usually approved a few years after the reference biologic product. In the past, the FDA approved a few biosimilars under the ANDA pathway, but these were not rated as therapeutically equivalent. The BPCI act established an approval process for biosimilars and the first biosimilar was approved in early 2015.

The Biologics Price Competition and Innovation (BPCI) Act was passed as part of the ACA and created an abbreviated licensure pathway for biosimilars to become interchangeable with an FDA-licensed biologic product. The legislation permits licensing to be awarded based on less than a full complement of product-specific preclinical and clinical data. The biosimilar must keep the same mechanism of action, route of administration, dosage form and strength as the reference product, and will only be approved for the indications of the reference biologic. In 2015, filgrastim-sndz (*Zarxio*), a leukocyte growth factor, became the first biosimilar approved in the United States. *Zarxio* can be therapeutically interchanged for *Neupogen*. These drugs are now listed in the FDA's *Lists of Licensed Biological Products with Reference Product Exclusivity and Biosimilarity or Interchangeability Evaluations*, commonly known as the *Purple Book*.

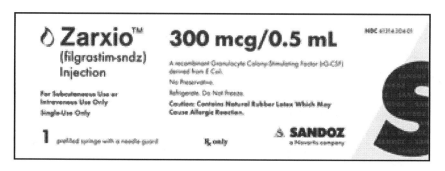

The package label for Zarxio, the first drug approved as a biosimilar in the U.S.

DRUG QUALITY AND SECURITY ACT OF 2013

The tragedy at the New England Compounding Center led Congress to pass the Drug Quality and Security Act (DQSA) as an amendment to the FDCA. One part of the legislation, section 503B, or the Compounding Quality Act, gave the FDA increased authority to regulate compounding. The law makes a distinction between traditional compounders and "outsourcing facilities". If a facility compounds sterile drugs for humans, they can register as an outsourcing facility under 503B. Drugs compounded by an outsourcing facility are exempt from the FDA new drug approval process and certain labeling requirements, but need to do the following:

- Comply with CGMP requirements

- Pay the FDA an annual fee of $15,000 and pay for inspections

- Report adverse events

- Provide the FDA with certain information about the products they compound

PREGNANCY AND NURSING LABELING FINAL RULE 2014

The drug labeling information requirements for pregnancy and nursing were changed in 2014. The previous Pregnancy Categories (A, B, C, D and X) will no longer be used and the information will be placed into new categories designed to provide more useful information of the health risks. The new requirements will be in package inserts by 2020. Drugs approved since June 30, 2001 will be required to use the new labeling requirements (see the figure). If the drug was approved prior to this date, the only change required in the labeling is to remove the letter category, and keep the previous information (the categories on the left of the graphic) the same.

The new information is placed into three categories:

- Pregnancy: Labor and delivery guidelines now fall under this category, which includes information for pregnancy exposure registries. The registries track data on the effects of certain medications on pregnant and breastfeeding women.

- Lactation: Previously labeled "Nursing Mothers," this category provides information such as how much drug is secreted through breast milk and the potential effects on a breastfed infant.

- Females and Males of Reproductive Potential: This is a new category that includes information on how a certain medication might affect pregnancy testing, contraception, and infertility.

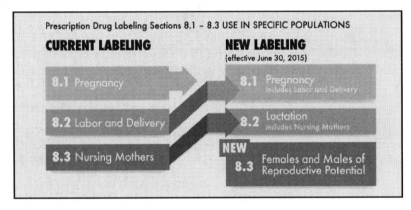

Changes to pregnancy categories.

NY: Triannual

Licensure, Registration, Certification and Operations

LICENSURE, REGISTRATION AND CERTIFICATIONS

Pharmacist

Requirements for a pharmacist license vary by state, and are set by the state's Board of Pharmacy. Select states issue pharmacist licenses from other agencies, such as the Health Department or the Consumer Protection Department. In most states, the legal age to become licensed is at least 18 years old; two states require a minimum age of 19 years,[6] a handful require a minimum age of 21 years[7] and one-third do not specify an age requirement. It is common to require a criminal history background check, which is sensible as the pharmacist has responsibility for drugs with abuse and diversion risk.[8]

If a licensed pharmacist would like to transfer his or her license to another state, the pharmacist must pass that state's version of the MPJE, except for the four jurisdictions that require an alternative (non-MPJE) law exam.[9] All states without exception require the applicant to pass the NAPLEX. Most states permit transfer of the NAPLEX score to another state within a year of passing the exam; a few states permit longer transfer periods or do not address the issue and may accept the transfer at any time at the discretion of the state board. The smallest state in the U.S., Rhode Island, has the shortest time period for NAPLEX score transfers (6 months). In addition to the NAPLEX and the MPJE or another state-specific law exam, a few states require a personal interview with the state board, and an additional compounding exam or some other type of practical exam.

---

6 Alabama and Wisconsin
7 Arkansas, Louisiana, Maine, Missouri, New York, Pennsylvania and Tennessee
8 A criminal background check is required in Arizona, Arkansas, California, Delaware, District of Columbia, Idaho, Indiana, Kentucky, Louisiana, Maine, Michigan, Mississippi, Missouri, New Jersey, Ohio, Oregon, Puerto Rico, South Dakota, Tennessee, Texas, Utah, Washington, Wisconsin and Wyoming.
9 Arkansas, California, Guam and Puerto Rico

License renewal is usually required every 2 years. If the license renewal is late beyond a certain date, the license will be not be active and the pharmacist will not be able to legally practice. The pharmacist will need to pay a fee to have the license reinstated, fulfill any continuing pharmacy education (CPE) requirements, and may need to retake licensing exam/s. The license renewal periods by state are listed in the table that provides the license renewal periods and the renewal due dates.

Continuing Pharmacy Education (CPE)

Education in pharmacy does not stop at the point of graduation. Pharmacists must be current with new drugs and with the changes in existing drug labeling and treatment guidelines. If this knowledge is lacking, the pharmacist will not be able to adequately assess the drug treatment and will lack expertise in advising patients and other healthcare professionals. Keeping current is an essential part of the professional practice of a pharmacist.

The professional licensing agencies are granting a license that certifies a minimum skill level and therefore require a certain number of CPE hours to be completed each license renewal cycle.[10] If the pharmacist is involved with a certain area of patient care (immunizations, HIV, others) there may be requirements for CPE in the area of expertise. Pharmacists can participate in live or correspondence (mail/Internet) CPE. A certain number of hours may need to be completed by attending a live program. In a few states the first license renewal cycle does not require CPE hours; the requirement is waived with the belief that the pharmacist is relatively current due to recent schooling, intern experience and preparation for the licensure exams. The CPE requirements by state are reviewed in the table on state-specific CPE requirements.

Foreign-Trained Pharmacists

Foreign-trained pharmacists must complete the Foreign Pharmacy Graduate Examination Committee (FPGEC) certification prior to applying for a license from the state in which they plan to practice. To achieve the certification, the pharmacist will need to pass two exams:

■ The Foreign Pharmacy Graduate Equivalency Examination (FPGEE), and

■ The Test of English as a Foreign Language (TOEFL)

Once the FPGEC certification is obtained, the foreign-trained pharmacist will complete the state's intern hour requirements, and take the NAPLEX and the state-specific law exams.

Name of agency issuing pharmacist licenses in your state: _op.nyed.gov_

Your state specific law exam if not (MPJE:) _____

List any other exam required for licensure: _Compounding exam_

---

10   *May be referred to as continuing education (CE) hours.*

List the time period permitted after the NAPLEX has been taken in which the score can be transferred to your state: _____

Pharmacist License Renewal Periods[11]

Pharmacists need to keep their license active in order to continue to practice. States select to require renewal every year, every 2 years, or every 3 years. The renewal will need to be sent in advance to allow time for processing. CPEs must be completed within the renewal cycle.

STATE	PERIOD	SPECIFIC YEARS	DUE DATE
Alabama	Biennial	Even years	31-Dec
Alaska	Biennial	Even years	Odd Years
Arizona	Biennial		31-Oct
Arkansas	Biennial	Odd Years	31-Dec
California	Biennial		Birthday Month
Colorado	Biennial	Odd Years	31-Oct
Connecticut	Biennial	Even years	31-Jan
D.C.	Biennial		28-Feb
Delaware	Biennial	Even years	30-Sep
Florida	Biennial	Odd Years	30-Sep
Guam	Biennial		30-Sep
Georgia	Biennial	Even years	31-Dec
Hawaii	Biennial		31-Dec
Idaho	Annual		30-Jun
Illinois	Biennial	Even years	31-Mar
Indiana	Biennial	Even years	30-Jun
Iowa	Biennial		30-Jun
Kansas	Biennial		30-Jun
Kentucky	Annual		28-Feb
Louisiana	Annual		31-Dec
Maine	Annual		31-Dec
Maryland	Biennial		Last day of birth month
Massachusetts	Biennial	Even years	31-Dec
Michigan	Biennial		30-Jun
Minnesota	Annual		1-Mar
Mississippi	Annual		31-Dec
Missouri	Biennial		31-Oct
Montana	Annual		30-Jun
Nebraska	Biennial	Even years	1-Jan
Nevada	Biennial	Odd Years	31-Oct
New Hampshire	Annual		31-Dec

11 State law information changes; updated tables are kept with the course video content and accessible when logged in from a computer.

STATE	PERIOD	SPECIFIC YEARS	DUE DATE
New Jersey	Biennial	Odd Years	30-Apr
New Mexico	Biennial		Last day of birth month
New York	Triennial	Birthday	Birthday month
North Carolina	Annual		31-Dec
North Dakota	Annual		1-Mar
Ohio	Annual		15-Sep
Oklahoma	Annual		Last day of birth month
Oregon	Biennial		30-Jun
Pennsylvania	Biennial	Even years	30-Sep
Puerto Rico	Triennial		Variable
Rhode Island	Annual		30-Jun
South Carolina	Annual		30-Apr
South Dakota	Annual		30-Sep
Tennessee	Biennial		Cyclical
Texas	Biennial		Last day of birth month
Utah	Biennial	Odd Years	30-Sep
Vermont	Biennial	Odd Years	31-Jul
Virginia	Annual		31-Dec
Washington	Annual		Birth date
West Virginia	Biennial		30-Jun
Wisconsin	Biennial	Even years	31-May
Wyoming	Annual		31-Dec

Continuing Pharmacy Education (CPE) Requirements*

STATE	REQUIREMENTS
Alabama	15 hrs/yr: 3 hrs live, Board-approved or ACPE-accredited
Alaska	30 hrs/2 yrs, ACPE-accredited
Arizona	30 hrs/2 yrs: 3 hrs law, ACPE-accredited or state CPE committee
Arkansas	30 hrs/2 yrs: 12 hrs live, 12 hrs ACPE-accredited, 2 hrs in immunization to retain competency, 3 hrs in senior care if applicable (nursing home pharmacist)
California	30 hrs/2 yrs, Pharmacy Foundation or ACPE-accredited. New licensees: 1st cycle exempt.
Colorado	24 hrs/yr by 10/31 license renewal in odd-numbered yrs, ACPE-accredited
Connecticut	15 hrs/yr (Jan-Dec), 5 hrs live, Board-approved or ACPE-accredited or Continuing Medicine Education (CME) or Nursing CE
D.C.	40 hrs/2 yrs: 10 hrs live, 2 hrs HIV, 2 hrs med errors, 2 hrs in immunization to retain competency
Delaware	30 hrs/2 yrs
Florida	30 hrs/2 yrs: 10 hrs live, 2 hrs med errors. 1 hr AIDS/HIV, 24 hrs for consultant pharmacist, 24 hrs for nuclear pharmacist
Guam	15 hrs/2 yrs, Board-approved
Georgia	30 hrs/2 yrs, by 12/31 of odd yrs, Board-approved or ACPE-accredited

STATE	REQUIREMENTS
Hawaii	30 hrs/2 yrs, ACPE-accredited, 1st year exempt
Idaho	15 hrs/yr: 12 ACPE-accredited or Continuing Medicine Education (CME), 3 hrs live, 1 hr law, 1 hr in immunization or sterile compounding to retain competency
Illinois	30 hrs/2 yrs, ACPE-accredited
Indiana	30 hrs/2 yrs: 6 hrs max in business or computer courses, 15 hrs Board-approved or ACPE-accredited
Iowa	30 hrs/2 yrs: 2 hrs law, 2 hrs med safety, 15 hrs ACPE-accredited in drug therapy, credits in 3 mths prior to renewal can be carried over
Kansas	30 hrs/2 yrs, board-approved
Kentucky	15 hrs/yr: Board-approved or ACPE-accredited
Louisiana	15 hrs/yr: 3 hrs live or 20 hrs total, ACPE-accredited
Maine	15 hrs/yr: 2 hrs must be in board-approved courses in drug administration
Maryland	30 hrs/2 yrs by last day of birth month prior to renewal, 2 hrs live, 1 hr med errors, 2 hrs for board meeting/4 hrs max
Massachusetts	20 hrs/yr: 2 hrs law, max 15 hrs correspondence (mail), max 8 hrs/day
Michigan	30 hrs/2 yrs: 10 hrs live, 1 hr pain
Minnesota	30 hrs/2 yrs
Mississippi	10 hrs/yr
Missouri	30 hrs/2 yrs
Montana	15 hrs/yr: 5 hrs live or 20 hrs total, Board-approved or ACPE-accredited or Continuing Medicine Education (CME)
Nebraska	30 hrs/2 yrs, ACCME, ACPE-accredited, Nebraska CPE
Nevada	30 hrs/2 yrs: 15 hrs accredited, 1 hr law, 3 hrs/full day board meeting
New Hampshire	15 hrs/yr: 5 hrs live, Board-approved (any board) or ACPE-accredited
New Jersey	30 hrs/2 yrs, submit proof, Board-approved or ACPE-accredited
New Mexico	30 hrs/2 yrs: 10 hrs live, 2 hrs opioids/patient safety, 2 hrs pharmacy law, ACCME, ACPE-accredited, residents take exam or attend inspector course in pharmacy law, non-residents take ACPE-accredited law course
New York	45 hrs/3 yrs renewal: max 22 hrs by correspondence/non-live, 3 hrs med errors, ACPE-accredited
North Carolina	15 hrs/yr: max 7 hrs non-live/correspondence, can carry over 5 hrs to next yr
North Dakota	15 hrs/yr: ACPE-accredited, can carry over 15/hrs to next yr
Ohio	60 hrs/3 yrs, 3 hrs in Board-approved law
Oklahoma	15 hrs/yr: accredited CPE, recommend 3 hrs live
Oregon	30 hrs/2 yrs: 2 hrs law, 2 hrs patient safety, 1 time 7 hrs pain CPE within 24 months of 1st license renewal, which includes 1 hr pain course by Pain Commission, Oregon Health Authority, and 6 hrs in pain management
Pennsylvania	30 hrs/2 yrs, 2 hrs patient safety (ACPE-accredited), 2 hrs injectable medications/biologics/immunizations if licensed in it, all ACPE-accredited, all pharmacists complete 2 hrs in child abuse/reporting during current renewal period
Puerto Rico	15 hrs/yr: 5 hrs live, 1 hr in immunization to retain competency
Rhode Island	15 hrs/yr: 5 hrs live, 1 hr in immunization to retain competency
South Carolina	15 hrs/yr: 6 hrs live, 7.5 hrs drug/patient management, ACPE-accredited, excess credits 1 year carry-over
South Dakota	12 hrs/in previous 24 months to registration renewal

STATE	REQUIREMENTS
Tennessee	30 hrs/2 yrs: 15 hrs live
Texas	30 hrs/2 yrs: 1 hr Texas pharmacy law
Utah	30 hrs/2 yrs: 12 hrs live, 15 hrs drug/patient management, 1 hr law/ethics, 2 hrs in immunization to retain competency, ACPE-accredited or by pharmacy professional associations or division
Vermont	30 hrs/2 yrs: 10 hrs live, 1st cycle exempt
Virginia	15 hrs/yr: 10 hrs live, new licensees: 1st cycle exempt, obtain and keep CE certificates/2 yrs
Washington	15 hrs/yr: ACPE-accredited or Commission-approved
West Virginia	30 hrs/2 yrs: 6 hrs live, 4 hrs immunization if immunizing pharmacist
Wisconsin	30 hrs/2 yrs, ACPE-accredited
Wyoming	12 hrs/yr, if inactive provide 5 yr CE prior to re-activation

*CPE	0.1 CEU = 1 hour of Continuing Pharmacy Education (CPE). Most states do not permit CPE hours in excess of the current period's requirements to be used for the next renewal cycle (carry over). If the state board permits carry-over it is noted in the table.
ACPE-accredited	The Accreditation Council for Pharmacy Education (ACPE) is the national agency for the accreditation of professional degree programs in pharmacy and for the providers of CPEs.
Board reviewed	The board or licensing agency can approve CPE programs; this may require submission and a fee.
1st year exempt	1st license renewal cycle post-graduation is exempt from CPE requirements.

Pharmacist Intern

Pharmacist intern experience provides real-life pharmacy practice exposure. The common requirement is to complete 1500 practice hours, with some exceptions. Some states permit hours to be obtained partially or solely as part of the PharmD curriculum in an American College of Pharmacy Education (ACPE)-accredited program. Refer to the table on the hours required in each state and the duration in which the internship remains active.[12]

States will require pharmacist applicants to register as pharmacist interns for this experiential learning. The term "experiential" refers to learning based on experience and observation, versus traditional classroom-style learning.

The intern hours are most commonly completed in pharmacies or as part of the school rotation experience. The American Association of Colleges of Pharmacy (AACP) task force on caring for the underserved has recommended that pharmacy students may fulfill intern hours when working under the direction of other healthcare professionals.[13] This recommendation does not correlate with most state board requirements. Several states permit interns to obtain hours (which will count towards licensure) in research or industrial settings under the supervision of non-pharmacist professionals.

---

12   Nebraska has eliminated the intern hour requirement, which is an unusual exception.
13   Zweber, A, Roche, VF, Assemi, M, et al. Curriculum Recommendations of the AACP-PSSC Task Force on Caring for the Underserved. Am J Pharm Educ. 2008 Jun 15; 72(3): 53.

The intern is a pharmacist in training and can perform the duties of a licensed pharmacist at the discretion of and under the supervision of a pharmacist. There may be exceptions; for example, the intern may not be permitted to have a key to the pharmacy. If the care that the intern is providing involves specialized training, such as administering immunizations, the pharmacist supervising the intern must also have received the specialized training or they will not be competent to provide supervision.

A state may permit the intern to counsel, which must be under the supervision of a pharmacist. Pharmacists are responsible for the work of the intern and thus there are ratios restricting the number of interns (and technicians) that the pharmacist can supervise.

Does the state permit interns to provide counseling? (Yes)/ No

Are there any limitations on the activities that an intern may conduct as compared to a pharmacist? _____

Provide the intern hours required in your state prior to sitting for the NAPLEX (see table):

__1040_____

Provide the duration of an intern registration (see table): _____

If the board specifies the type of hours required list them: _____

What is the ratio of interns for each pharmacist in a community setting: _____

What is the ratio of interns for each pharmacist in a hospital setting: _____

Are there permitted conditions in which the number of interns per pharmacist can increase? Yes / No

If yes, list the conditions under which this is permitted: _____

Does the state require the intern to submit a fingerprint card?   Yes / No

Does the state require the intern to have a criminal background check? Yes / No

Pharmacist Intern Hour Requirements

STATE	HOURS REQUIRED
All states not listed	1500
Arkansas	2000
District of Columbia	1500 independent/1000 ACPE accredited
Florida	2080
Idaho	None
Illinois	400
Maryland	1560 foreign/1000 ACPE accredited
Michigan	1600
Minnesota	1600
Mississippi	1600
Nebraska	None
Nevada	1740
New Jersey	1440
New York	1040
Oregon	1440
South Dakota	2000
Tennessee	1700
Utah	1740
Vermont	1740
Wyoming	1200

Intern License Expirations

STATE	INTERN LICENSE EXPIRATION
Arkansas, Connecticut, Delaware, Florida, Hawaii, Minnesota	6 months following post-graduation or when licensed as a pharmacist, whichever comes first
Guam, Idaho, Illinois, Indiana, Maine, New Hampshire, New Mexico, North Dakota, Ohio, Rhode Island (expires on 6/30), South Dakota, Washington, West Virginia, Wyoming (expires on 9/30)	1 year
District of Columbia, Iowa, Louisiana, Montana	1 year post-graduation
Nebraska	15 months post-graduation
Alaska, Maryland, Missouri, New Jersey, Oregon	2 years
California	1-6 years
Colorado	2 years, expires on 10/31
North Carolina, Tennessee	Not specified
Mississippi, Nevada	4 years
Georgia, Massachusetts, Michigan, New York, Oklahoma, Utah, Vermont	5 years
Texas	6 months post-graduation; intern hours expire 2 years after completion
Kansas, Kentucky, Pennsylvania, South Carolina	6 years
Arizona	Must be actively attending pharmacy school to apply, maximum 6 years

Pharmacist Preceptor

The preceptor is a licensed pharmacist who mentors pharmacist interns during their college of pharmacy's introductory and advanced pharmacy practice experience, and when completing the intern hours required for licensure as a pharmacist. This is a "service-learning" experience: the intern is expected to provide service (i.e., work at the pharmacy) in conjunction with an experience that is designed to teach the intern about their chosen profession. Practice settings vary and in optimal circumstances the intern hours should be completed in various settings with preceptors who have the time and willingness to provide mentorship. At the current time, the employment market for intern experience is limited and the majority of interns will find work in just one type of practice setting.

Preceptors require state registration in about half of the states and in the other half all that is required is an active pharmacist license in good standing. A few states require the training site (i.e., the pharmacy) to register with the board. States have set a maximum number of interns that can be supervised by each pharmacist at one time.

Circle if your state requires preceptors to register with the state board. (Yes) No

List any additional requirements in your state to become a preceptor: *1 yr. working as a pharmacist +, active license*

Pharmacy Technician

Pharmacy technicians have been assisting in the pharmacy throughout the history of the profession. Previously, training was done on the job for the type of help the pharmacist required. The first formal technician training programs were developed in hospitals by the American Society of Hospital Pharmacists (ASHP) in order to enable the technicians to perform accurate calculations and prepare sterile medications. Training is now required in most practice settings.

Technician Registration

Most states require registration with the state board for the primary purpose of having the applicant attest that they have not been convicted of a felony or misdemeanor and that they have not been involved in any criminal actions with controlled or non-controlled drugs. For the registration to be approved the agency will usually conduct some type of investigation, such as a criminal background check and/or drug screening. It is common for states to require that the technicians be at least 18 years old, have a high school diploma or general equivalency degree (GED), and lack a criminal history.

Technician Licensure

Seven states grant professional licenses to technicians.[14] Licensure is more involved than registration and will include requirements such as work experience, some type of examination, and education, such as a technician training program or graduation from a college of pharmacy.

14   *Alaska, Arizona, California, Indiana, Oregon, Utah and Wyoming.*

Technician Certification

Currently, most technicians are not certified on a nationwide basis. This is changing as technicians are taking on more complex tasks to allow pharmacists to devote more time to patient care activities. In August of 2014, the NABP published the *Model State Pharmacy Act* with the goal of assisting the state boards by defining basic requirements for various issues concerning pharmacy practice.[15] This document included an important discussion on the expanding role of technicians, and the requirements for certification. All technicians can enter prescriptions into the computer and assist with drug storage, insurance claim processing and cashiering. Certification enables the technician to be involved with limited patient care activities, which can include receiving new written or electronic prescriptions (this is permitted in select states only),[16] transferring prescriptions, and compounding. Technicians who are certified will need to complete continuing education hours in order to retain the certification.

The two primary certification exams are the Pharmacy Technician Certification Board's (PTCB) Pharmacy Technician Certification Examination and the National Healthcareer Association's (NHA) ExCPT Pharmacy Technician Certification Exam. In states that have both certified and non-certified technicians the certified technicians have a higher degree of responsibility, which can include supervisory responsibility over other technicians.

Fourteen states have initiated "tech check tech" (TCT) programs where one technician checks the work of another technician, such as in prescription preparation.[17] TCT programs are expanding due to the increase in prescription volume and the increase in pharmacist responsibilities. The ASHP Pharmacy Practice Model Initiative Summit recommended that technicians should be more routinely involved with distributive functions that do not require clinical judgment.[18]

What is the minimum age in which a person can become a pharmacy technician in your state? 18 _____

Activities beyond those discussed above that are permitted for non-certified technicians in your state: _____

_____

List any exams or certifications required for all technicians: _____

_____

---

15   *The Model State Pharmacy Act and Model Rules of the National Association of Boards of Pharmacy (Model Act).* http://www.nabp.net/publications/model-act. (accessed 2015 Jun 17).

16   *Illinois, Iowa, Louisiana, Massachusetts, Michigan, Missouri, New Hampshire, North Carolina, North Dakota, Rhode Island, South Carolina and Tennessee.*

17   *California, Colorado, Idaho, Kansas, Kentucky, Michigan, Montana, North Carolina, North Dakota, Oregon, South Carolina, Texas, Utah and Washington.*

18   *ASHP Pharmacy Practice Model Summit Recommendations.* http://www.ashp.org/menu/AboutUs/ForPress/PressReleases/PressRelease.aspx?id=625 (accessed 2015 Aug 4).

If your state has a basic level of technicians and higher level of technicians, list the higher level designation here and identify the training or examination required:

_____

What is the ratio of technicians for each pharmacist in a community setting:

1:2
_____

What is the ratio of technicians for each pharmacist in a hospital setting:

_____

Are there permitted conditions in which the number of technicians per pharmacist can increase? If yes, list the conditions under which this is permitted:

_____

Controlled Substance Registrants

DEA registration is required for the manufacture, distribution, research, prescribing and dispensing of controlled substances.

Individual persons or facilities will require DEA registration. For example, a physician will require a DEA number in order to be authorized to write prescriptions for controlled substances. The pharmacy or hospital will require DEA registration in order to receive, store and dispense the controlled substances. Individuals or facilities that have registered with the DEA are referred to as registrants.

Individuals and institutions (including prescribers, hospitals and pharmacies) submit the DEA Form 224 to apply for a DEA number.[19] There are different registration forms for companies involved with the manufacturer or distribution of drugs and for other types of organizations that require controlled substances.

The authority to manufacture, distribute, prescribe or dispense non-controlled drugs comes from the state in which the facility or practitioner is licensed. The state license is obtained first, before registering with the DEA.

DEA registration Renewals are sent 60 days prior to expiration in order to provide ample time to complete & process.

---

19   DEA Form 224 New Application for Registration is at: http://www.deadiversion.usdoj.gov/drugreg/reg_apps/224/224_instruct.htm (accessed 2015 Aug 6).

Specialty Pharmacist

The term specialty pharmacist is used for three different purposes:

1. For the purpose of the law exam, the term is most likely referring to any state-mandated requirements for pharmacists who participate in specialized patient care services. The requirements vary, and pharmacists who register for state approval (such as with a certification) may be able to advance their career options, receive a differential in salary and/or improve their job satisfaction.

    There are different organizations that provide certification and not all are recognized by each board of pharmacy. For example, the Ohio Board of Pharmacy recognizes the Board of Pharmacy Specialties (BPS) Certifications, the Certified Specialist in Poison Information and the Commission for Certification in Geriatric Pharmacy. California, which has pharmacist provider status, has set criteria for the Advanced Practice Pharmacist (APP), which requires work experience and training.

2. A specialty pharmacist can refer to pharmacists trained in a specific area of patient care, usually achieved through post-PharmD residency training and/or through work experience. The pharmacist may not be required to register with the board and may be hired based on their special skill set. The ability of a specialist to focus on a select group of drugs in their specialty (versus the thousands of drugs available) enables the pharmacist to become a specialist and apply advanced knowledge to their practice specialty.

The Pfizer Guide on Careers in Pharmacy lists these specialties:[20]

Compounding Pharmacist	Nutrition Support Pharmacist
Consultant Pharmacist	Oncology Pharmacist
Critical Care Pharmacist	Operating Room Pharmacist
Drug Information Specialist	Pediatric Pharmacist
Hospice Pharmacist	Pharmacogenomics Pharmacist
Hospital Staff Pharmacist	Pharmacy Benefit Manager
Hospital Clinical Pharmacist	Poison Control Pharmacist
Industry-Based Pharmacist	Primary Care Pharmacist
Infectious Disease Pharmacist	Psychiatric Pharmacist
Long-term Care Pharmacist	Public Health Service Pharmacist
Managed Care Pharmacist	Regulatory Pharmacist
Military Pharmacist	Veterinary Pharmacist
Nuclear Pharmacist	

Pharmacy specialists not listed above include Advanced Practice Pharmacist, Emergency Department (ED) Pharmacist, Informatics Pharmacist, Transplant Pharmacist, Pain Management Pharmacist, Pharmacist Editor and Nephrology Pharmacist. In some states the designation permits the pharmacist to initiate and adjust certain medications, with or without a physician-directed agreement that will be outlined in a protocol.

20 *The Pfizer Guide to Careers in Pharmacy. Pfizer Pharmaceuticals Group, Pfizer Inc.: New York, NY; 2002.*

3. The term "specialty pharmacist" is used to refer to pharmacists who work in "specialty pharmacies," which are closed-door pharmacies (i.e., not open to the public) that mail specialty drugs to patient's homes. The majority of drugs dispensed in this manner are high-cost biologics. Counseling is provided by telephone.

If pharmacist specialists require specific registration in your state, list the specialist classifications, the requirements and the privileges that come with a classification:

_____

_____

_____

_____

DISCIPLINARY ACTIONS AGAINST PHARMACY STAFF

ACTION	DESCRIPTIONS
Suspended	License is inactive; may be reinstated after conditions are met (e.g., completion of pharmacist recovery program, probation)
Revoked	License is taken away by the licensing agency
Reinstated	License that was taken away is given back, in active status
Surrendered	Individual agrees to voluntarily gives up licensure, often with compulsion in order to avoid penalties and/or criminal charges

In most states, the board of pharmacy has responsibility for initiating action against a pharmacist who is deemed unfit to practice for a limited period, or on a permanent basis. The board may have delegated this authority to a division within the board, such as the Board's Quality Assurance Committee. There are some jurisdictions where this responsibility rests with another agency. The most common causes of disciplinary action are impairment, theft and diversion.[21]

Since the board in each state is primarily concerned with the health of the public, they have instituted policies to prevent personnel from working in pharmacies who have been involved with drug diversion, including requirements for background criminal checks and/or a requirement for urine screening. Leniency may be extended to an individual with drug addiction if the licensee is willing to enroll in a rehabilitation program, which are described in the next section. Drug abuse and addiction can involve prescription drugs, illicit drugs and alcohol.

21   Nebraska: Department of Health and Human Services, Division of Public Health; Guam: Board of Examiners for Pharmacy; New York: Board of Regents; Utah: Division of Occupational and Professional Licensing; Wisconsin: Pharmacy Examining Board.

The board (or other designated regulatory agency that manages disciplinary actions), has the final authority over disciplinary proceedings, which can involve license probation, suspension or revocation. If the activity involves criminal actions, such as drug diversion or other types of theft, the matter will need to involve law enforcement. Pharmacies can also lose the license to operate: for example, if a pharmacy is found to be operating as a "pill mill", where excessive and inappropriate opioid prescriptions are routinely filled, the pharmacy may have the state license to operate (and the pharmacy's DEA registration) revoked.

RECOVERY PROGRAMS FOR DRUG AND ALCOHOL ABUSE OR PSYCHOLOGICAL ILLNESS

Addiction is an occupational hazard in pharmacy due to the stress involved with this type of work and the easy access to drugs. The drug abuse rate among pharmacists is thought to be about twice as large as the general population. Pharmacists who abuse drugs may falsely believe that their own clinical knowledge will somehow prevent them from developing dependence. This belief is inaccurate. Substance use among pharmacists can jeopardize the public health; compounding or dispensing errors resulting from the impairment can cause injury, including death. A concurrent psychological illness will put the person at a higher risk for addiction and will require separate treatment, which may be available under the individual's health insurance coverage or may need to be paid for out-of-pocket. The goal of the board or other licensing agency, if no serious offense has been committed, is to assist the pharmacist in obtaining treatment and returning to practice.

The purpose of a pharmacist recovery program is to develop a treatment plan, monitor participation and provide encouragement and support. In the quickest, most confidential and least stressful manner possible, the individual receives the proper help to face the problem, deal with it and, if possible, return to the profession as a contributing member.

The goal is recovery and rehabilitation.

Colleagues who refer coworkers for help remain confidential.

The majority of the state programs are available for all licensed healthcare professionals. Physicians and nurses have similar abuse concerns, including high stress levels at work and easy access to drugs. The state board or regulatory agencies financially sponsor these programs, and there are no dues or costs for the individual to participate. The only requirement for voluntary enrollment is a desire to seek help and maintain recovery. The enrollment may be involuntary when it is part of a disciplinary action.

If a pharmacist is known to be impaired at work, it is a requirement of the other licensees at the pharmacy to report the suspected person to the state board, and possibly to law enforcement if theft has occurred. The board may elect to offer the licensee a path to treatment with or without license probation or suspension, depending on whether an incident, such as a dispensing error, was involved, and if the licensee is a repeat offender. If theft of a controlled substance was involved, the repercussions will be more severe and would likely include license revocation.

If a license has been revoked for drug abuse or any other threat to public safety, the pharmacist can apply to the state board or licensing agency for reinstatement, which may or may not be granted. The board has broad discretionary options to determine if the license should be reinstated. If the agency is convinced that the person involved is rehabilitated, reinstatement may be possible; if the agency views the person as a continued threat to public safety, it is likely to deny the reinstatement request.

My state provides an impaired pharmacist recovery program.   Yes / No

Name the organization that operates the program: _____

List who can enroll in the state's program: _____

What are the enrollment conditions? _____

Can a pharmacist enroll themselves? _____

RENAMING, RELOCATING, OR CLOSING A PHARMACY

A change of business name, closure or relocation of a pharmacy will require notification to the state board within a set time limit, which will be short, such as "immediately" or "within 30 days". Many states require inspection of the new site prior to approving a relocation request. In some jurisdictions all that is required is a notification of the move to the state board, which is made by completing a change of address form.

The DEA will require a notice of change of the address of the registrant when scheduled drugs are moving location, such as with relocation. If the pharmacy is transferred to another owner, an inventory of the controlled substances must be taken on the day the drugs are moved, either before the day's shift has started, or at the end of the day. Schedule II drugs will require completion of a DEA Form 222 (or the electronic CSOS equivalent) when the drugs are changing location. The transfer of schedules III-V drugs must be documented in writing to show the drug name, dosage form, strength, quantity, transfer date, and the names, addresses, and DEA registration numbers of the parties involved in the transfer.

In my state, pharmacy closures must be reported to the state board within this number of days: _____

INSPECTION OF A PHARMACY

State boards hire pharmacists (and in some states, non-pharmacists) to inspect pharmacies and make sure that the store is in accordance with federal and state laws and regulations. The list of the items inspected is long, and includes everything from recordkeeping requirements in accordance with the controlled substances act to the temperature of the refrigeration units. The pharmacy will be subject to minor or major infractions if the requirements are not met. Most states provide self assessment (or "self-inspection") forms for the pharmacist-in-charge to use to identify deficiencies and correct them, preferably prior to an announced or unannounced inspection. The completion of these forms may be required on a scheduled basis. The self-assessment/self-inspection form is useful for board study; these include the legal requirements that the state board feels is important, and which may be tested on the state's pharmacy law exam. There may be separate forms for the outpatient community pharmacy setting, inpatient setting and forms for pharmacies involved with sterile compounding.

The name of the inspection or assessment form/s used by the pharmacists in my state:

_____

If the form must be completed on a scheduled basis, list the time period: _____

Who is responsible for completing this form? _____

Is the form sent into the board or kept at the pharmacy? _____

How long must the pharmacy keep the form?_____

DRUG SUPPLY CHAIN INTEGRITY

The FDA requires that manufacturers, repackagers and pharmacies that are registered with the FDA as outsourcing facilities follow Current Good Manufacturing Practice (CGMP) requirements. CGMPs are designed to ensure drug identity, strength, quality and purity. Examples of CGMPs include the requirement to use only quality raw materials and reliable testing procedures.

The term "wholesaler" refers to the intermediary company in the drug distribution chain who receives the drugs from the manufacturer, and distributes them to the individual pharmacies. Prescription drugs must be purchased only from licensed drug distributors. The license must be current in each state/s in which the wholesaler operates. The wholesaler's state license is obtained from the state board of pharmacy, with a few exceptions.[22] Drugs can be obtained from wholesalers located in the same state as the pharmacy, and from out-of-state wholesalers, which are also licensed by the boards of pharmacy in most states.[23] Medical devices such as ostomy supplies and some diabetes supplies (lancets, test strips

22   The state board of pharmacy is responsible for licensing in-state wholesale distributors in all states except Connecticut, District of Columbia, Florida, Illinois Louisiana, Nebraska, New Jersey, North Carolina, Pennsylvania, Puerto Rico, Texas and Utah. In these jurisdictions another state agency is responsible for issuing the wholesaler license.
23   An agency other than the state board of pharmacy is responsible for licensing out-of-state wholesalers in Alaska, Guam, Hawaii, Massachusetts and Utah.

and meters) are commonly sold in pharmacies. Some of the devices require a prescription, which is called an order by the Centers for Medicare and Medicaid Services (CMS). Many states set a limit on the number of syringes that can be purchased without a prescription. [24]

Does your state set a limit of the maximum number of syringes that can be purchased at one time without a prescription? (Yes) / No ~~H~~

If yes, list the number _#10   with ID_

SPACE AND EQUIPMENT

A facility that stores and distributes prescription drugs should be in accordance with the standards set by USP, which include requirements on the facility size, construction and storage space. There must be a separate (quarantined) storage area for counterfeit/adulterated/expired drugs. The space must be maintained in a clean and orderly condition, be free from rodent and vermin infestation, be in a commercial location, have restricted access, and include inventory controls to identify theft and diversion. Individual state boards of pharmacies can mandate requirements for additional specifications.[25]

If sterile medications are prepared they must be prepared in a laminar flow hood and/or biological safety cabinet with a fume hood. Other equipment which may be required include a dose calibrator, an analytical balance, a lead-shielded drawing station (if involved with radiopharmaceuticals), assorted glassware, a microscope, a thermometer, refrigeration equipment, syringes, decontamination supplies, transport and packing material, and any other required supplies. Instruments must be calibrated at scheduled times and documentation on the calibration history should be available in the pharmacy.

The self assessment/inspection form will include space requirements that are specified by the state.

List any state-specific pharmacy space requirements: —————————————————

TEMPORARY ABSENCE OF THE PHARMACIST

Fatigue resulting from continuous physical and mental activity can cause lapses in attention to critical details, and this can lead to dispensing errors. An increasing number of states have attempted to address the issue of scheduled breaks for pharmacists. This is challenging in pharmacies that have one pharmacist on duty at certain times; without this person present, essential work, including dispensing new prescriptions and counseling patients, is shut down. Several of the states specify additional restrictions if one pharmacist is on duty alone. Any additional state-mandated breaks will be posted online.

---

24   Most states require a license for distributors of medical devices that require a "prescription" order; states that do not require a license for this purpose include Arkansas, Colorado, Delaware, Florida, Georgia, Hawaii, Idaho, Illinois, Indiana, Massachusetts, Minnesota, Mississippi, Missouri, Nebraska, New Mexico, North Carolina, Washington, West Virginia and Wyoming. Alaska and Kentucky require the license for in-state distributors only (not out-of-state). Rhode Island requires the license only if the device contains a prescription drug.
25   USP Chapter 1079, available at www.usp.org

STATE	RESTRICTIONS FOR TEMPORARY ABSENCE OF PHARMACIST
Alabama, California, Massachusetts	If one pharmacist: may leave pharmacy open if controlled substances are secured. Only refills can be provided to patients (if they have been visibly checked by the pharmacist) and only if counseling is not required. Break is limited to 30 minutes, if store is without a pharmacist. The pharmacist can leave the store during the break. Technicians and interns can continue to work, and the pharmacist will check the work upon return. P&P required.
D.C.	If one pharmacist, the pharmacy must close during meal times and breaks.
Florida	Break is limited to 30 minutes, if store will be without a pharmacist. If a sign is posted that the pharmacy is open at that time the pharmacist must remain on the premises and be available to counsel, if requested. If patient requests counseling and the pharmacist is not available, the pharmacist should contact the patient/s at the earliest available time. Technicians can continue to work if the pharmacist remains on the premises and is available to respond to questions. The pharmacist will check the work upon return.
Massachusetts	If one pharmacist: may leave pharmacy open if controlled substances are secured. Only refills can be provided to patients (if they have been visibly checked by the pharmacist) and only if counseling is not required. Break is limited to 30 minutes, if store will be without a pharmacist. The pharmacist can leave the store during the break. Technicians can continue to work, and the pharmacist will check the work upon return. The pharmacy manager can develop a P&P to permit PTCB and/or board-certified technicians and interns to receive telephone prescriptions.
Mississippi	Periodic breaks are permitted to "relieve fatigue and mental and physical stress".
Montana	If one pharmacist: may leave pharmacy open if controlled substances are secured. Only refills can be provided to patients, if they have been visibly checked by the pharmacist, and only if counseling is not required. A sign displaying the scheduled break time/s must be prominently posted. Break is limited to 30 minutes. The pharmacist must remain on site during the break. Support personnel can continue to work. If more than one pharmacist on the shift the breaks must be staggered. P&P required.
New Jersey	Break is limited to 30 minutes for a meal, and additional "restroom" breaks. The pharmacist must remain on site during the break. A sign must be posted that the pharmacist is on break but available for emergencies and counseling. Support personnel can continue to work.

STATE	RESTRICTIONS FOR TEMPORARY ABSENCE OF PHARMACIST
North Carolina	A pharmacist cannot work longer than a 12-hour shift per day. If working 6 continuous hours, a 30-minute and a 15-minute break must be provided.
Oregon	There must be appropriate opportunities for uninterrupted rest periods and meal breaks.
Tennessee	There may be one temporary absence of a pharmacist not exceeding 1 hour per day. A sign that says "Pharmacist not on duty" must be prominently posted. No medication may be dispensed. The prescription area must be closed off by a floor to ceiling barrier.
Vermont	If one pharmacist: may leave pharmacy open if controlled substances are secured. A break is required if shift is more than 8 hours. The break time should be consistent. Only refills can be provided to patients, if they have been visibly checked by the pharmacist, and only if counseling is not required. Refills can be taken over the phone. New prescriptions cannot be taken over the phone in the absence of a pharmacist. Written prescriptions can be taken from patients. A sign displaying the scheduled break time/s must be prominently posted. Break is limited to 30 minutes. The pharmacist must remain on site during the break. If more than one pharmacist on the shift the breaks must be staggered. Policy and procedures are required.

Permissible pharmacist breaks and maximum durations in my state: _____

_____

Must a sign be posted that the pharmacist is not on duty?   Yes / No

Activities that are restricted during the absence of a pharmacist: _____

_____

ADVERTISING AND SIGNAGE

The state board may have requirements and restrictions on advertising and signage. Commonly, a "Notice to Consumers" is required that includes information such as the right to counseling, what should be known about the drug/s prior to leaving the pharmacy, and the availability of interpreter services for patients with limited English proficiency.

NABP recommends that three items be displayed in the pharmacy, which may have been adopted by your state:

1.   If the pharmacy is involved with radiopharmaceuticals, radiation caution signs should be posted throughout the restricted area.

2.   Biohazard caution signs should be properly used and posted throughout the appropriate area/s.

3.   Appropriate notices to employees are posted.

List if your state has advertising limitations or signage requirements.

_____

_____

_____

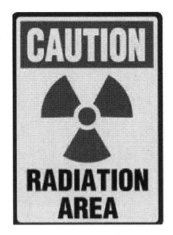

Signage indicating radiation is present due to the presence of radiopharmaceuticals.

PHARMACY SECURITY

All pharmacists on duty are responsible for the security of the pharmacy, including effective control against theft and diversion. The space must be secured by a physical and/or electronic barrier which can be locked and, preferably, be able to identify entry at all times. Access to non-pharmacy personnel should be kept to a minimum and any entry of non-pharmacy staff will be at the discretion of the pharmacist. Security systems should include protection against outside and inside theft, including theft of electronic information and patient records. Safe practices to reduce risk and respond safely during a robbery are discussed in the pharmacy practice section.

To maintain the security and confidentiality of patient records, the computer system must have safeguards for entry. The system must be backed up and the prescription order information should be available quickly; the NABP recommends a 2-hour time period to retrieve back-up prescription data. An auxiliary system must be used to store refill information. When the computer system has been down (i.e., not operable) and comes back up and operable, all prescription information that has been manually recorded during this time should be entered promptly.[26] In the event that the prescription information is permanently lost, the board of pharmacy should be notified.

---

26   The NABP, in the Model Act, recommends that all information recorded manually during a lapse in the computer system should be entered within 96 hours from the time the system is back up and operable.

POLICIES AND PROCEDURES

The majority of states require every pharmacy to have a current policy and procedures (P&P) manual. A policy is a course of action for a specific activity and the procedure (written into the policy) includes the steps involved that must be carried out by the staff. It's a "what to do" for the various expected and unexpected events that occur in a pharmacy. P&Ps help keep the pharmacy running efficiently. The manual can protect the pharmacy in case of litigation and may be required for state or insurance company reimbursement.

Select states will require pharmacists to prepare P&Ps for all pharmacy operations and others identify the types of P&Ps required. All P&Ps must conform to federal and state laws and regulations.

LIBRARIES

A pharmacist should keep a current copy of the state laws and regulations, USP reference chapters, reference texts specific to the type of work performed (for example, radiopharmaceutical reference sources if involved in nuclear pharmacy), and current drug information resources. Every state permits the use of electronic reference materials, with a few state-specific requirements.[27]

DISPLAY OF LICENSES

All facilities must publicly display or have readily available all licenses of the licensed personnel.

Does your state require licenses to be displayed in public view?   Yes / No

DRUG STORAGE IN A PHARMACY SETTING

Controlled Substance Storage

The DEA requires that controlled substances be kept in a securely locked cabinet of "substantial construction". This means that the cabinet should not be easy to break apart in order to access the contents. Another option that is acceptable is to partially conceal the controlled drugs by dispersing them throughout the stock of non-controlled drugs. For example, *Ambien* could be placed on the shelf in alphabetical order with the other drugs beginning with the letter A.

---

27   *South Dakota requires the printed version of the reference sources be kept in the pharmacy. Maryland permits electronic resources to be used as supplements to the printed versions, and only if the site is created by a reputable medical publisher that is recognized as a standard for that type of information. Massachusetts permits electronic resources if they are updated at least quarterly. Guam and South Carolina do not address the issue of electronic reference sources.*

Investigational New Drug Storage

Investigational drugs must be stored in a location that has limited access and in accordance with instructions from the supplier, including any required storage conditions. This means that the drugs must be "quarantined" (separated) from other drug stock. Documentation should be maintained for each transport, handling and receipt of the study drugs. Any breach in practice must be reported to the investigator.

Repackaged and Resold Drug Storage

The FDA defines repackaging as the "act of taking a finished drug product from the container in which it was distributed by the original manufacturer and placing it into a different container without further manipulation of the drug". Pharmacies repackage drugs in both hospital and community settings in order to meet the needs for unit-dose dispensing, to prepare smaller doses of medications that are not commercially available, and to repackage a large container into smaller sizes for dispensing purposes. On occasion, a pharmacy may repackage smaller containers into larger containers to manage a shortage.

If the drug being repackaged is an FDA-approved drug, the repackaged drug is assigned a beyond use date (BUD) that will be in accordance with the dates provided in the USP guidance. These are discussed in the pharmacy practice section. If the expiration date on the original (larger) container that was repackaged is a shorter time period than the BUD recommendation in the USP, the shorter time period from the original container must be used.

Expired (Outdated) Drugs and Drug Sample Storage

Expiration dates are estimated in a conservative manner using FDA-mandated stability testing. The manufacturer will not make recommendations regarding product use beyond the expiration date, based on legal and liability concerns, and pharmacies must follow the same procedure because the FDCA prohibits the sale of expired prescription and non-prescription drugs.

Expiration date requirements extend to free drugs provided to charities or non-profit medical clinics, and to drug samples. It is not acceptable to dispense or send out any expired drugs, even if they are provided at no cost. If drugs are provided to charitable or non-profit organizations, the charity or non-profit must agree to send to disposal or return any drugs that become expired while in their possession. Drugs that have become expired must be quarantined from the rest of the drug stock in labeled containers prior to return or disposal. Prescription drug samples, whether expired or not, cannot be stored at or distributed from a retail pharmacy at any time.

Drug Recalls

The actions on getting the recalled drug back should correlate with the severity of the recall. If the recall involved specific batches or lot numbers, the pharmacist will need to have the stock checked and pull the recalled drug. It is often the person responsible for drug purchases that identifies the lots involved and the locations of the recalled drug.

Pharmacies must be positioned to received notification of recalls from multiple sources, which includes the FDA, federal, state or local law enforcement, and manufacturers or repackagers. If there are multiple locations in a central facility, the pharmacists involved with the recall will need to identify where the drug is located, and remove it from all patient care areas and storage locations, including in ADCs. If patients have received the drug, it may be necessary to send urgent mailings with the envelope stamped "drug recall" and marked "urgent" in bold red letters. If the drug has been taken by the patient, the prescriber will be involved with any corrective action. The pharmacy staff may be asked to identify alternative treatments.

When the recalled drug is returned to the pharmacy it is quarantined (separated) from other drugs prior to being returned or destroyed. Drugs that are quarantined for any reason (recalls, adulteration, expiration) must be labeled appropriately and placed in separate containers. Otherwise, they may be sent to the wrong location, or accidentally dispensed.

A P&P describing the procedure for managing drug recalls is required and will include providing written documentation on the disposition of the drugs. The documentation must be kept for the state's required period, which will be 2 or more years.

Recalls are carried out by the manufacturer, as the FDA generally lacks the immediate legal authority to simply require a manufacturer to recall the drug. Recalls may be initiated by FDA request, by an FDA order under statutory authority or at the company's own initiative. There are times when the FDA is slow to act and the company will pull the drug first to avoid patient harm and probable lawsuits.

CLASS	DESCRIPTION
Class I Recall	A situation in which there is a reasonable probability that the use or exposure will cause serious adverse health consequences or death. For example, a morphine tablet manufactured with ten times the amount of active ingredient.
Class II Recall	A situation in which use or exposure can cause temporary or reversible adverse health consequences or where the probability of harm is remote. For example, ketorolac injections have been recalled in 2010 and 2015 due to the possibility of particles in the vials.
Class III Recall	A situation in which use of or exposure is not likely to cause adverse health consequences. For example, the coloring on tablets may have been applied inconsistently.

DRUG DELIVERY

Drug Delivery through the Mail or by a Pharmacy Employee

There are few limitations imposed by states on drug delivery services besides the need to provide a toll-free phone number (with stated hours) for the patient or their agent to use if they wish to receive counseling or have drug-related questions. Insurance plans favor home delivery due to decreased costs. Patients on chronic medications who make multiple trips to the community pharmacy may find home delivery more convenient, especially when the patient has difficulty with movement or transportation.

It is permissible according to federal law to mail scheduled and non-scheduled drugs; the outer packaging cannot indicate the contents.

There are several large companies that deliver medication through the mail in many states, such as *Express Scripts*. There are smaller companies that work with different insurance plans to deliver medications in daily or weekly dose packs for patients that need help with adherence, which is discussed further.

Under the CSA, it is acceptable to deliver controlled substances through the U.S. Postal Service (USPS). The CSA does not specify by name other common carriers, such as FedEx. There are no restrictions on the use of common carriers stated under the CSA. The carrier, in some cases, may have set their own limitations. *No signiture required.*

When sending drugs by mail delivery, the outside packaging should not contain any identifiable marks that could be used to indicate the contents. The inner labeling must have the required labeling in accordance with federal and state labeling requirements. The restrictions for safe packaging imposed by the Poison Prevention Packaging Act apply to the containers inside the package.

If a pharmacy employee has attempted delivery to a patient's work or residence and the patient refused delivery or the employee was not able to find the location, the drug can be returned to stock if it has not left the control of the pharmacy, which means that the contents must have remained in the manufacturer's original, sealed, and tamper-evident bulk, unit-of-use, or unit-dose packaging or the dispensing pharmacy's original packaging, and was returned to the pharmacy within the same day as the unsuccessful delivery attempt.

If your state has set limitations on medication delivery (by couriers, pharmacy employees, or by kiosk dispensing) list the limitations here: _____

_____

Vacuum Tubes

Vacuum or pneumatic tubes are used for drug delivery in many hospitals. Tube delivery systems vary in the shape and size of the tube and in the transport force and speed. In any setting, limitations on the use of vacuum tubes for this purpose can be due to hazards created by the drug itself or drug decomposition that can occur during the delivery process. Drugs that are not safe to deliver by tube at any time include:

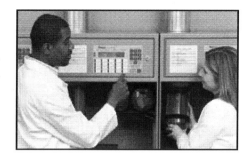

Preparing pneumatic tubes used for drug delivery.

- Hazardous compounds, including chemotherapy.

- Combustible products, including some gels and sprays.

- Protein products, which can become damaged from agitation (such as insulin and immunoglobulins).

Each facility will need to develop guidelines in a P&P that will include a list of drugs that should not be delivered by this method. If a specific drug is not mentioned, and there is a lack of guidance on whether a drug can be delivered safely by this method, it will be left to the pharmacist's judgment to decide whether the tube delivery is acceptable. If there is doubt for a particular drug, the tube delivery should not be used.

Drive-Up Windows

Pharmacies with drive-up (also known as drive-through) windows are convenient for patients to pick up medications. However, there are limitations with dispensing drugs through a window, including difficulty providing confidential counseling, the inability to open a container to discuss the contents, and the inability to provide a demonstration of the use of non-oral medications, such as inhalers.

A pharmacist assisting a patient at a drive-up window.

The window imposes a barrier to the pharmacist's ability to assess the patient for "red flags" of drug diversion. A few state boards have issued limitations on the use of drive-up windows. For example, Delaware permits schedule II prescriptions to be dropped off at a drive-up window, but requires the filled prescription to be picked up inside the pharmacy.

If your state has issued limitations on drive-up windows list them here: _____

DRUG PARAPHERNALIA

The U.S. Justice Department defines drug paraphernalia as "any equipment that is used to produce, conceal, and consume illicit drugs". Examples of drug paraphernalia include pipes and bongs for inhaling marijuana smoke, cigarette papers, and freebase kits or other equipment used for crushing and preparing injections from oral formulations.

Drug paraphernalia cannot be sold in pharmacies.

QUALITY ASSURANCE AND MEDICATION ERROR REPORTING

The most common error made by pharmacists is giving the wrong drug to a patient.

There are other types of errors, including dose calculation errors. The boards of pharmacy have requirements for each store to maintain a Continuous Quality Improvement (CQI) program, which is followed when a medication error occurs. The medication error is referred to as the Quality-Related Event (QRE). The CQI program requires a P&P that must be followed when a medication error has occurred. This will include conducting a "root cause" analysis, which is a retrospective analysis of the steps that led to the QRE.

The CQI program should include:

- Designated individuals responsible for the program, including implementation, maintenance and monitoring.

- A set time frame under which the CQI is initiated after the QRE has occurred. NABP recommends that the investigation be initiated within 3 days and individual state boards may have a more stringent requirement of 1 or 2 days.

- Formulation of a plan to amend the pharmacy system and workflow to avoid a repeat of the same or similar type of QRE, based on the data provided by the CQI.

- Any required changes in the pharmacy systems and workflow processes.

- Education to the staff, performed on a continual basis, on safe practices. Lessons learned from the CQI must be passed on to the rest of the pharmacy team.

NABP recommends that each pharmacy conduct a self-audit at least quarterly to determine if QREs have decreased and a survey of the customers (or a sampling of the customers) at least annually to help determine patient perception of the pharmacy's quality.

NOTIFICATION OF POTENTIAL TERRORIST EVENTS

Pharmacists were involved in New York City in the management of patients injured or exposed to chemicals in the wake of the September, 2001 attacks. Since that time, the American Pharmacists Association (APhA) has developed recommendations for pharmacists to respond in the case of a terrorist event. This includes developing an alert system to notify staff and patients of such an event, plans to move affected persons to safety and to notify pharmacists who may be involved as first responders or as members of medical teams. Pharmacies may have to relocate temporarily or may need to supply medication to patients who are not their usual customers, but are unable to enter or reach their originating pharmacy. The pharmacy's terrorist attack response plan should be included in the P&P manual. Emergency dispensing requirements are described further.

REPORTING PHYSICAL ABUSE

Pharmacists are mandatory reporters of child abuse and neglect.[28] Mandatory reporters have regular contact with vulnerable people such as children, disabled persons, and senior citizens, and are therefore legally required to report suspected or observed abuse to an appropriate agency, such as social services, law enforcement, or the state's toll-free reporting hotline. Reports provided to the hotline may be made anonymously. A report should be made when the pharmacist, acting in his or her official capacity, suspects or has reason to believe that a child is a victim of abuse or neglect. The Patient Care and Affordable Care Act of 2010 included a provision to expand elder abuse legislation from a state to a national level; this has been slow to implement, and some states have enacted legislation to require mandatory reporting of suspected elder abuse independently.

TREATMENT FOR TUBERCULOSIS

Tuberculosis treatment is complex, and challenging. Treatment of active disease is long-term (6 months to 2 years, depending on the level of resistance), which can result in adverse consequences, including hepatic and ocular damage. The adverse effect of neuropathy from isoniazid use can be alleviated with pyridoxine (vitamin B6) if the pharmacist is aware of the requirement and provides the patient with the correct vitamin and encourages adherence. There is a high risk of drug interactions due to the strong in-

Directly observed therapy (DOT)

ducing effect of the common agent rifampin, and more modest interactions with other drugs in the regimen. Tuberculosis drugs have to be taken in a consistent manner (such as without food, daily, or 2-3 times weekly) in order to be effective. The pill burden is high, which makes adherence challenging. Yet, adherence is essential due to multidrug resistance and the health consequences from inadequate treatment.

---

28   https://www.childwelfare.gov/pubPDFs/manda.pdf (accessed 2015 Aug 1).

Patients may be in the lower economic strata and may not have the time or financial resources to devote to adequate treatment. In select pharmacies the pharmacists participate in directly observed treatment (DOT) in which patients come to the pharmacy two or three times weekly to take their medication in front of the pharmacist. The patient may be encouraged to attend with an incentive, such as a small amount of money. In Indiana, a successful DOT program resulted in a decline in the rate of TB and reduced the incidence of drug resistant cases. DOT is now the standard of care for tuberculosis treatment in the state. Pharmacies are located in the community and provide an ideal location for DOT administration. Several states with high disease incidence currently have pharmacists participating in observing DOT.

Pharmacy Practice

This section reviews federal law for dispensing prescriptions and primarily covers non-controlled substances. The laws and regulations for controlled substances are more stringent and are reviewed in the next section.

FUNDAMENTAL RESPONSIBILITIES OF THE PHARMACY STAFF

The Pharmacist

The pharmacist is responsible for supervising the daily operations of the pharmacy to ensure that all activities in the pharmacy are performed safely, in compliance with the law, and without risk of harm to patients.

The traditional role of a pharmacist is the safe and proper dispensing of medications. When a pharmacist signs off on a prescription container or IV bag, the pharmacist is confirming that the dispensed medication matches the prescription and the safety risks have been evaluated, including allergies, adverse events, and drug interactions. For compounded preparations, the quality of the product is the legal responsibility of the pharmacist, not the technician who prepared the product, since the pharmacist is responsible for supervising the staff. The pharmacist's designation on the compounded product indicates that the pharmacist has verified that the compounded product was made correctly. The technician can still face consequences for careless work or legal action if any illegal activities (such as theft) have taken place.

Pharmacists have the discretion to decide on the best course of action for a patient, based on his or her professional judgment. This includes decisions on whether to fill a prescription when the prescriber cannot be reached, or whether a prescription should be filled at all.

As of late 2015, provider status for pharmacists had been approved on a state-by-state basis and national legislation was pending. This status enables pharmacists to receive compensation for the clinical services they provide.

In some states, an additional designation, the advanced practice pharmacist (APP), which enables pharmacists to provide clinical services in various settings under collaborative practice agreements (CPAs). The role of APP is similar to that of clinical pharmacists, and in each position the responsibilities depend on the pharmacist's skills and the arrangements at the facility. Historically, and in the absence of provider status, clinical services have been performed under a CPA.

My state permits pharmacists to perform clinical activities, which include: _____

_____

To perform clinical requirements these conditions should be met: _____

_____

My state has an advanced practice pharmacist (APP) designation. Yes / No

If yes, list the requirements for this designation and the tasks permitted: _____

_____

_____

A collaborative practice agreement is a formal practice relationship between a pharmacist and another healthcare provider, in which the healthcare provider makes a diagnosis, supervises the patient care, and refers patients to the pharmacist to provide patient care services and collaborative drug therapy management (CDTM). The CDTM will include the initiation, modification, and monitoring of the drug therapy. The patient care services typically include the ability to perform physical assessment and order the labs required to monitor the drugs.

The National Alliance of State Pharmacy Associations (NASPA) conducted a survey on the variability between state CPAs, which was reported by APhA in October 2014.[29] The survey results reported on the status of CPAs in each state:

- 38 states allow pharmacists to initiate drug therapy.

- 45 states allow for the modification of existing drug therapy (Florida pharmacists are permitted to initiate a defined list of drugs without a CPA).

- 29 states require the drugs and disease states that the pharmacists manage to be specified.

---

29   Available at http://www.pharmacist.com/policy-101-collaborative-practice-empowers-pharmacists-practice-providers (accessed 2015 Jul 11).

The Pharmacist-in-Charge

A pharmacy must have a pharmacist-in-charge (PIC) that is responsible for the daily operations of the pharmacy. The daily responsibilities for staff pharmacists and the PIC can overlap, but the PIC has the final responsibility. The PIC makes sure that the pharmacy is compliant with federal and state law. The PIC's license can be jeopardized (warnings, suspension or revocation) if inappropriate or illegal actions occur at the PIC's store, including a lack of counseling, manufacturing posing as compounding, drug diversion, and improper staff ratios.

Although the purpose of having a PIC is to make sure the store is operating legally, this does not diminish the legal responsibility of the individual staff pharmacists. However, if a store is found to be missing a substantial amount of a controlled substance over a period of time, if records are not being stored properly, or if controlled substance inventories are not performed when required, it is the PIC who will answer to the state board of pharmacy.

State boards can have additional regulations regarding the PIC, such as:

- Limiting the number of pharmacies for which the PIC is responsible for supervising.

- Setting a maximum physical distance permissible between pharmacies if the PIC is responsible for more than one location.

- Requiring a minimum number of hours that a PIC must be present at the pharmacy.

- Requiring a pharmacist to complete a minimum number of years of experience as a staff pharmacist in order to be eligible to become a PIC.

My state permits a PIC to be in charge of more than one pharmacy: Yes / No

If yes, list the number of stores a PIC can manage: _____

List any maximum driving distance permitted between pharmacies: _____

The Pharmacist Intern

A pharmacist intern is training to become a pharmacist and can perform all functions of a pharmacist at the discretion of and under the supervision of a pharmacist, with a few state-specific exceptions. Your state may have set limitations, such as prohibiting the intern having a key to the pharmacy, prohibiting interns from administering vaccines, or prohibiting interns from transferring controlled substance prescriptions. Only the pharmacist and the pharmacist intern can take new prescriptions over the phone. The ratio of how many interns can be supervised by one pharmacist varies by state. Some states allow pharmacies to have more pharmacist interns present than the legal limit as long as the intern is only performing technician or clerk functions. List your state restrictions and ratios:

Intern restrictions (versus what a pharmacist can perform): _____

_____

Ratio in hospital setting: 1 pharmacist to _____ intern/s.

Ratio in community setting: 1 pharmacist to _____ intern/s.

My state allows additional pharmacist interns present at any given time as long as the intern is only performing technician or clerk functions.   Yes / No

The Pharmacy Technician

Pharmacy technicians are permitted (with some state exceptions) to perform the following tasks while under the direct supervision of a pharmacist:

■ Enter prescriptions into the pharmacy computer.

■ Package prescriptions, which include removing drugs from stock, counting drugs, placing drugs into containers, and labeling the container.

■ Call prescribers for refill authorizations.

■ Compound medications.

■ Transfer prescriptions.

■ Permit one technician to check the work of other technicians (rather than having the pharmacist check the technician's work) in a Tech Check Tech (TCT) arrangement.

■ A handful of states permit technicians to accept called-in prescriptions from a prescriber's office in a hospital and/or community pharmacy.

My state permits technicians to accept new prescriptions over the phone. Yes / No

List the practice site and other requirements in your state for the technicians (such as training required or certification) and setting type if Tech Check Tech is permitted.

_____

Most states have a ratio of how many pharmacy technicians can be supervised for each pharmacist on duty. This varies from one pharmacist for each two technicians, to any number that the pharmacist feels they are reasonably able to supervise, which is always at the pharmacist's discretion.

Ratio in hospital setting: 1 pharmacist to _____ technician/s.

Ratio in community setting: 1 pharmacist to _____ technician/s.

Is there an exception in the state law that permits additional technician/s to be present in the pharmacy at any given time, such as having the technician perform some type of repetitive task (e.g., adherence packaging)?

_____

The Pharmacy Clerk

Clerks are non-licensed personnel with no specific training required. The clerk is often the person accepting prescriptions at the "drop off" window, verifying the patient's insurance coverage, and completing the transaction at the point of sale or the "pick up" window. The clerk is permitted to type prescriptions into the pharmacy computer and the pharmacist will verify that it matches to the actual prescription. Depending on state law, clerks can request and receive refills. A clerk cannot stock or pull medications from the shelves or package prescriptions. A clerk is not allowed to handle prescription medications other than at the point of sale.

My state permits clerks to request and receive refills.   Yes / No

Clerks cannot be subject to license suspension or revocation since clerks do not have a professional license. The pharmacist supervising the clerk is responsible for ensuring that the work meets the requirements of federal and state law. There are no maximum limits on the number of clerks allowed to be in the pharmacy at one time. There can be as many clerks as the pharmacist feels they are reasonably able to supervise, which is always at the pharmacist's discretion.

REQUIREMENTS FOR VALID PRESCRIPTIONS

Written, Oral, Electronic, and Faxed Prescriptions

The Durham-Humphrey Amendment of 1951 authorized dispensing of medications pursuant to a valid written prescription, or an oral prescription, which is immediately reduced to writing (i.e., is written on a prescription form). With the advent of technology, states passed their own laws that permit faxed, and subsequently, electronic prescriptions.

A prescription should minimally contain the following:[30]

■ Patient's full name, date of birth, and street address

■ Prescriber's name, license designation, address

■ Name, strength, dosage form, and quantity of drug prescribed

■ Directions for use

■ Refills authorized, if any

■ Date of issuance

■ Prescriber's signature

No Rx from online websites!

Healthcare Providers Authorized to Prescribe Medications

Healthcare practitioners who are licensed by law to prescribe medications can include physicians (MD, DO), dentists, podiatrists, veterinarians, nurse practitioners, pharmacists, optometrists, and naturopathic doctors. Independent and collaborative prescribing authority varies greatly by state. Before dispensing a medication, the pharmacist must make a good faith effort to determine that the prescription is valid, which includes having been written by a valid prescriber.

Physicians have unlimited, independent prescribing authority in every state while all other prescribers can only prescribe within their scope of practice and/or under a physician directed protocol. For example, a naturopathic doctor would be limited to natural drugs (and possibly epinephrine due to anaphylaxis risk), a dentist can prescribe medications related to the oral cavity and dental procedures, and an optometrist can prescribe medications related to ocular conditions.

Valid Prescriber/Patient Relationship

In order to fill a prescription, a prescriber/patient relationship should exist. The NABP has clarified that each of these conditions should be met for the prescription to be considered valid:[31]

1.   A patient has a medical complaint.

2.   A medical history has been taken.

---

30   *The Model State Pharmacy Act and Model Rules of the National Association of Boards of Pharmacy (Model Act). http://www.nabp.net/publications/model-act. (accessed 2015 Jun 17).*

31   *Same as above.*

3.   A face-to-face physical examination adequate to establish the medical complaint has been performed by the prescribing practitioner or through a telemedicine practice approved by the appropriate practitioner board.

4.   A logical connection exists between the medical complaint, medical history, the physical examination and the drug prescribed.

Self Prescribing and Prescribing for Family Members

Although not specifically addressed by the DEA, the American Medical Association (AMA) recommends against physicians treating oneself or immediate family members. There are ethical limitations involved with self-treatment and with the treatment of family members: the prescribers may not be able to objectively and adequately interview, examine, order diagnostic tests or drugs or counsel themselves or their family members due to personal relationships. There is also the potential for drug diversion.

Treating oneself or immediate family members can be prohibited by the state medical board in which the prescriber is licensed. Some states limit this type of prescribing to medical emergencies or for short-term, minor issues. Some states prohibit physicians from prescribing certain categories of drugs to oneself or to family members, such as schedule II drugs or all controlled drugs. Additionally, insurance companies may not provide coverage for treatment of oneself or known relatives. Federal law requires that all prescription medications be prescribed only in the context of a valid prescriber-patient relationship, which should include a written record of the encounter, such as a chart note. The same limitations on physicians that are set by the states and insurance companies commonly extend to the mid-level practitioners. In states that do not limit or have partial limitations on this type of prescribing, the pharmacist will need to make a judgment call on whether or not to fill such a prescription.

My state board sets limits on prescribing controlled drugs to oneself or family members. Yes / No
If yes, state the limitations: _____

_____

My state board sets limits on prescribing non-controlled drugs to oneself or family members. Yes / No
If yes, state the limitations: _____

_____

Prescriptions from Retired or Deceased Prescribers

Federal law does not specify whether a prescription remains valid after it is discovered that the prescriber has become retired or deceased. In some states, the prescription will be invalid under state law. In other states, there is a lack of guidance on the matter, therefore it would not be against the law to refill prescriptions from retired or deceased prescribers. If there is no guidance from the state, then by default the pharmacist may use his or her discretion when deciding to fill or refill a prescription written by a retired or deceased prescriber.

If the prescriber is no longer practicing, the pharmacist should encourage the patient to look for a new prescriber as soon as possible and not to wait until the prescription is expired or the refills are exhausted. If another prescriber takes over the deceased prescriber's practice, the patient may be able to obtain a new prescription from the prescriber who took over the practice.

My state does not permit new prescriptions or refills to be filled if the prescriber is known to have become deceased.   Yes / No

Prescriptions from Other States or Territories

In most cases, a prescription written by an out-of-state prescriber in a different U.S. state or territory is valid if a true prescriber/patient relationship is present. States can have specific rules for out-of-state prescription, such as requiring the out-of-state prescription to meet the requirements for in-state prescriptions or only allowing non-controlled substances to be filled for out-of-state prescriptions. Puerto Rico and Guam do not permit pharmacists to fill out of state prescriptions for controlled substances.

Prescriptions from Foreign Countries

Except for a couple of states that permit the practice, a pharmacist may not fill prescriptions from other countries. Whenever a prescription is filled, the prescription must meet the state's requirements, such as the requirement for security forms.

Off-Label Promotion by Manufacturers

The drug manufacturer (i.e., the "drug reps") cannot initiate conversations with other healthcare providers regarding off-label use for one of their drugs. The manufacturer and their representatives may discuss off-label use if a healthcare practitioner has voluntarily, on their own initiative, requested the information.

Off-Label Prescribing

Off-label use means that the drug will be used for a purpose for which the drug is not indicated. Indicated uses have been approved by the FDA, and will be listed in the package insert. Off-label use also includes using the drug for the indicated condition, but in a different patient population. If a drug has been FDA approved for at least one indication, prescribers are legally allowed to prescribe it for any other reason they feel is both safe and effective for the patient's health condition. Off-label prescribing is common and is often beneficial. There may be medical literature to support the off-label use, and the use may even be included in clinical guidelines. Occasionally, the off-label use is inappropriate and unsafe.

Pharmacists are legally permitted to fill prescriptions for off-label indications. The pharmacist must use his or her professional judgment when filling off-label prescriptions. Prior to filling a prescription for an unfamiliar off-label use, the pharmacist should attempt to find out if the drug has been studied for that purpose, if it is likely to be efficacious, and if it appears safe for the patient. The pharmacist can research the use and/or request supporting literature from the prescriber.

CORRECTING ERRORS AND OMISSIONS ON PRESCRIPTIONS

An omission is a type of error in which required information on a prescription has been left out, such as the number of tablets required. Errors on a prescription for non-controlled drugs can be revised by the pharmacist if the error is minor, such as misspelling the drug name. If the error is not minor, the pharmacist should consult with the prescriber, and document the discussion, including the agreed to change/s. Alternatively, after verification with the prescriber, the prescription can be re-written as an oral prescription. In some cases, the original prescription will be voided and the prescriber will resend another prescription by fax or electronic transmission.

Correcting errors and omissions on prescriptions for controlled substances is stricter and is discussed in the controlled substances section.

PRESCRIPTION REFILLS

Refills of prescriptions are permitted as long as the refills were authorized orally or in writing by the prescriber, however the amendment did not specify time limits. The majority of states allow prescriptions to be refilled up to 1 year from the original issue date. Wyoming and South Carolina allow prescriptions to be refilled for up to 2 years and a handful of states (including Georgia and New York) do not specify a time limit. This will depend on the pharmacist's judgment or individual store policy. Refills for schedules III and IV have shorter time limits (6 months) in which refills are permitted relative to non-controlled drugs, and some states have limits on the number of total day supply the refills can provide.

Schedule V refills are either handled the same way as schedules III and IV refills, or with the same requirements for non-controlled refills depending on the individual state. Federal law prohibits refills of schedule II drugs. Refilling controlled substances are further discussed in the Controlled Substances chapter.

In my state, refills of non-controlled prescriptions must be filled within this time period from the issue date: _____

In my state, refills on schedules III and IV prescriptions must be filled within this time period from the issue date: _____

My state specifies a day's supply maximum for schedules III and IV. Yes / No. If specified, list the maximum day's supply: _____

My state treats refills on schedule V prescriptions differently than refills for non-controlled medications. Yes / No. If schedule V refills are handled differently, list the difference/s:

the same as C III - IV time limit (6 months)

EMERGENCY REFILLS WITHOUT THE PRESCRIBER'S AUTHORIZATION

Some states allow emergency refills without the prescriber's authorization if the prescriber is unavailable to authorize the refill and, if in the pharmacist's professional judgment, failure to refill the prescription might interrupt the patient's ongoing care and have a significant adverse effect on the patient's well-being. The pharmacist must have made a reasonable effort to contact the prescriber. The pharmacist must use caution that the emergency filling was medically necessary.

Limitations on emergency filling will vary from state-to-state. Some states allow emergency refills for non-schedule drugs and schedule III-V drugs. Other states only allow emergency refilling of non-scheduled drugs. Schedule II drugs are prohibited from having refills. The emergency days' supply to be dispensed varies by state; this is typically 72 hours but can be up to a one-month supply. The emergency refill must be properly documented and an original prescription for the emergency filling must be obtained in a timely manner. Federal law prohibits refills on schedule II drugs and emergency fills of schedule II medications must have at least the prescriber's oral authorization. This is discussed further in the controlled substances section.

My state allows emergency filling of non-controlled drugs without the prescriber's authorization.   Yes / No

My state allows emergency filling of schedule III-V drugs without the prescriber's authorization.   Yes / No

My state allows an emergency supply of medication for this amount of days: _____

If your state has additional restrictions on emergency filling, and states a time period in which to receive the prescription from the prescriber, list the restrictions/time limit:

_____

PRESCRIPTION TRANSFERS

There are no federal limitations on the transfer of non-controlled prescriptions and, unless limited by state law, a pharmacist can transfer the prescription as long as there are refills remaining. The transfer must be directly communicated between two pharmacists (or certified pharmacy technicians, in states that permit this practice).

The pharmacist or certified pharmacy technician who transfers the prescription to another pharmacy must write or stamp "void" on the face of the prescription (front side). The name and address of the pharmacy to which the prescription is transferred to, the name of the pharmacist receiving the prescription, and the transfer date is written on the back of the prescription.

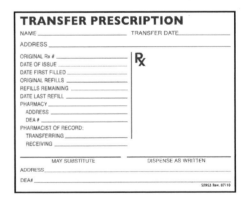

The pharmacist at the store receiving the transferred prescription will use a blank form to record the information.

NY only ①refill at a time can be transferred.

The pharmacist or certified pharmacy technician that receives the prescription reduces it to writing and writes "transfer" on the face of the prescription, along with the information that is required for a prescription. Many pharmacies have transfer forms that have "transfer" preprinted on the top.

INFORMATION REQUIRED ON MULTIPLE UNIT (MULTIPLE DOSE) PRESCRIPTION LABELS

Multiple unit containers are the typical prescription containers dispensed to patients in the outpatient and community settings. These are usually given as a 30 or 90-day supply. The Durham-Humphrey Amendment exempts dispensing pharmacists from meeting most of the requirements that manufacturers must meet for container labeling except:

Requirements from the Durham-Humphrey Amendment

- The label most not be false or misleading

- The drug dispensed must not be an imitation drug

- The drug must not be sold under the name of another drug

- The packaging and labeling must conform to the official compendia standards

- If the drug is susceptible to deterioration, it must be packaged and labeled appropriately

Federal law requires the following information on the dispensed prescription label:

- Name and address of dispenser
- Serial or prescription number
- Date of filling
- Prescriber's name
- Patient's name
- Directions for use
- Cautionary statements

Some states require additional information on the prescription label such as:

- Date of initial fill
- *(NY)* Name of the dispensing pharmacist ✓
- Business hours
- *(NY)* Pharmacy phone number
- Expiration date of drug ✓
- Drug name and strength ✓
- Address of patient ✓
- Name of the manufacturer or distributor ✓
- Lot or control number
- Physical description of drug (e.g., oblong ivory tablet 73 00 logo)
- Refills remaining ✓

FORMATTING STANDARDS FOR MULTIPLE UNIT (MULTIPLE DOSE) PRESCRIPTION LABELS

USP 17 on Prescription Container Labeling is the official standard for prescription format, appearance, content and language instructions. The goal of standardizing the labels is to promote patient understanding of medication usage, increase adherence, and reduce medication errors. These standards do not apply to inpatient medications since those are pursuant to medication orders, and are labeled for a healthcare professional to administer.

The content of the prescription container label is often the only drug information the patient will read. Thus, it has to be easy to understand and must include the proper auxiliary labels. The label should only include the most important information needed for safe and effective use. Too much information is not acceptable because the important details can be overlooked.

The prescription directions should follow a standard format so the patient is accustomed to finding the information each time a prescription is received. The text should be in horizontal direction only. For added emphasis, the label can highlight critical information in bold typeface or color, or use white space to set off the items listed.

The following critical items should be prominently displayed in a large font size (e.g.,12-point Times Roman or 11-point Arial):

1.   Patient name

2.   Drug name (brand and generic) and the drug strength

3.   Explicit, clear directions for use, in simple language

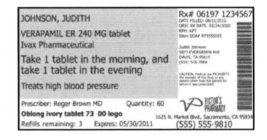

All other, less critical information should not distract from the more important information listed above. Less critical information should be placed away from the items above (e.g., at the bottom of the label or in another less prominent location) to avoid distracting from the key information. If the indication for the drug is indicated on the prescription, then it should also be included on the prescription label unless the patient wishes otherwise.

Directions for use should be clear and easy to interpret. Time periods should be specified and numbers should be used instead of alphabets when appropriate. For example, rather than "Take two tablets twice daily" the label should read "Take 2 tablets in the morning and 2 tablets in the evening." Avoid hourly intervals (such as "every 8 hours") since this requires the patient to count. In general, specifying an exact time should be avoided except if required for drugs that must be taken at exact times (e.g., tacrolimus for a transplant patient, with times specified on the prescription, 12 hours apart). Specifying an exact time can be too restrictive for patients who are busy with work, school, or other responsibilities. Jargon or Latin terminology should not be used. When possible, directions for use should be in the patient's preferred language if it is not English.

Auxiliary labels should be evidence-based and written in simple language for key warnings. They should be placed in a standard place on the label and should be provided for each and every prescription as needed, and not at the discretion of the pharmacist. See the dispensing controlled substances section for more information on the labeling for scheduled drugs.

My state requires tablet identification (the description, such as number, shape and color) on the container label.   Yes / No

My state requires the pharmacy to include their phone number on the container label. (Yes) / No

My state requires the ability to provide patients with visual impairment a larger container label type size, such as 12-point san serif type.   Yes / No

My state requires that the critical information on a container label be printed in at least 12-point san serif type for all patients. (Yes) / No

My state requires critical information on the label to be bolded or printed in color ink (circle if either bold or color ink is specified).   Yes / No

EXPIRATION DATES VERSUS BEYOND-USE DATES

The expiration date listed on the manufacturer's drug container identifies the time during which the prescription drug will still meet the requirements of the USP monograph, as long as it is kept in appropriate storage conditions in the original sealed container. The expiration date will usually be notated with a month and year, and the drug is acceptable to use until the end of the month in which it expires. For example, if the expiration date is 3/2016, then the last date of use should be March 31, 2016.

The pharmacist must determine a suitable beyond-use date which is considered the date that the patient should no longer use the medication. The pharmacist should indicate this date on the prescription container. Depending on state law, the beyond-use date may or may not be the same as the manufacturer's expiration date. The beyond use date is never greater than the manufacturer's expiration date. The monographs for some preparations state how the labeled expiration date shall be determined. For example, the beyond-use date for reconstituted *Augmentin* suspension is 10 days.

Unless otherwise specified in the individual monograph (such as with the *Augmentin* suspension) or in the absence of stability data to the contrary, the beyond-use date for a multiple unit container is no later than either of the following:[32]

■ The expiration date on the manufacturer's container, or

■ One year from the date the drug is dispensed, whichever is earlier

What if the drug product does not have an expiration date? Then it is considered misbranded, may be considered expired, and should not be dispensed.

CHILD-RESISTANT PACKAGING

Prior to implementation of the Poison Prevention Packaging Act (PPPA), accidental poison exposure was a leading cause of injury in children less than 5 years old. There was no standard way to protect children from ingesting common dangerous substances, including drugs and household substances. The PPPA requires the use of child-resistant (C-R) containers for most over-the-counter, prescription drugs, and dangerous household chemicals. Child-resistant containers are designed so that 80% of children less than 5 years of age cannot open it while at least 90% of adults can.

The PPPA mandates that a new plastic container and closure must be used for each prescription dispensed. This is done to avoid wear and tear damage, which can reduce the C-R effectiveness of the container. If a glass container is used, only the top plastic closure needs to be replaced. Reversible containers (child-resistant when turning the closure one direction, but not child-resistant in the other direction) are permitted if dispensed in the child-resistant mode, but are not recommended.

Similarly, the patient or the prescriber may ask the pharmacy to package prescription drugs in an "easy open", non-child-resistant container. The prescriber can waive the use of a child-resistant container for a single prescription at a time. The patient can provide a blanket waiver for all dispensed prescriptions. The pharmacist should document the waiver request with the patient's signature.

Child-resistant packaging is also exempt if the drug is to be administered directly by a healthcare provider to a patient.

For the benefit of elderly and handicapped patients who might have difficulty opening C-R containers, the PPPA allows manufacturers to package one size of an OTC product in a noncompliant "easy open" container as long as the same product is also available in a C-R container. The package must have the warning "This package is for households without young children" or "Package Not Child-Resistant."

---

32   *USP Chapter 7, on Labeling, available at www.usp.org*

Drugs That Require C-R Packaging

- All oral prescription drugs (not oral inhalers and not topical drugs that are applied inside the mouth, with the exception of oral anesthetics)

- Liquid anesthetics such as lidocaine and dibucaine (*Nupercainal*), OTC NSAIDs, including salicylates

- Any OTC iron supplement, multivitamin/mineral with iron and natural products with iron

- Loperamide (*Imodium*)

- Minoxidil (*Rogaine*)

- Prescription drugs that were converted to OTC

- Mouthwash, including fluoride-containing mouth rinses

- Oral and non-oral investigational drugs for outpatient use, with an exception for drugs packaged in unit-dose if there is data that the amount being used would not cause harm to a young child if ingested; these are for patients who are enrolled in a clinical drug trial

Drugs That Do Not Require C-R Packaging

- Sublingual dosage forms of nitroglycerin

- Sublingual and chewable forms of isosorbide dinitrate in dosage strengths of 10 milligrams or less

- Erythromycin ethylsuccinate granules for oral suspension and oral suspensions in packages containing no more than 8 grams of the equivalent of erythromycin

- Cyclically administered oral contraceptives in manufacturers mnemonic (memory-aid) dispenser packages that rely solely upon the activity of one or more progestogen or estrogen substances

- Anhydrous cholestyramine in powder form

- All unit-dose forms of potassium supplements, including individually-wrapped effervescent tablets, unit-dose vials of liquid potassium, and powdered potassium in unit-dose packets, containing no more than 50 milliequivalents of potassium per unit-dose

- Sodium fluoride drug preparations including liquid and tablet forms, containing no more than 110 milligrams of sodium fluoride (the equivalent of 50 mg of elemental fluoride) per package or no more than a concentration of 0.5 percent elemental fluoride on a weight-to-volume basis for liquids or a weight-to-weight basis for non-liquids and containing no other substances

- Betamethasone tablets packaged in manufacturers' dispenser packages, containing no more than 12.6 milligrams betamethasone

- Pancrelipase preparations in tablet, capsule, or powder form and containing no other substances

- Prednisone in tablet form, when dispensed in packages containing no more than 105 mg of the drug, and containing no other substances

- Mebendazole in tablet form in packages containing no more than 600 mg of the drug, and containing no other substances

- Methylprednisolone in tablet form in packages containing no more than 84 mg of the drug and containing no other substances

- Colestipol in powder form in packages containing no more than 5 grams of the drug and containing no other substances

- Erythromycin ethylsuccinate tablets in packages containing no more than the equivalent of 16 grams erythromycin

- Conjugated Estrogens Tablets, USP, when dispensed in mnemonic packages containing no more than 32 mg of the drug and containing no other substances

- Norethindrone Acetate Tablets, USP, when dispensed in mnemonic packages containing no more than 50 mg of the drug and containing no other substances

- Medroxyprogesterone acetate tablets

- Sacrosidase (sucrase) preparations in a solution of glycerol and water

- Hormone Replacement Therapy Products that rely solely upon the activity of one or more progestogen or estrogen substances

- Colesevelam hydrochloride in powder form in packages containing no more than 3.75 grams of the drug

- Sevelamer carbonate in powder form in packages containing no more than 2.4 grams of the drug

Electronic cigarettes (e-cigs) may require C-R packaging in the near future. There has been an increase in emergency room visits and poison control center phone calls after young children had accidently ingested electronic cigarettes due to its artificially sweet flavorings (e.g., apple, vanilla, strawberry).

SINGLE DOSE (UNIT-DOSE) PRESCRIPTION LABELS

Drugs packaged as unit-doses are convenient for hospitals and skilled nursing facilities because it reduces drug diversion, drug waste, and medication errors. The unit-dose container is a non-reusable container designed to hold a quantity of drug intended for direct, oral administration as a single dose. Unit-dose packaging can be performed by the drug company or prepared from multiple dose containers in the pharmacy. A benefit of unit-dose packaging is that if the drug is not used and the container is intact, the drug can

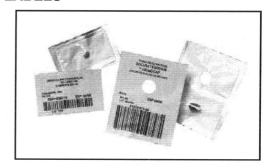

Unit dose packages prepared in a hospital pharmacy, from multiple dose containers.

be returned to pharmacy stock and re-dispensed. Pharmacies repackage drug from multiple dose containers into unit-dose packaging for administration to patients in facilities such as hospitals on a routine basis; it is important to know the requirements for the unit-dose label listed below in order to repackage the drug.

Unit-dose packaging reduces medication errors. Before administering the drug, the nurse scans the barcode on the patient's wristband and the unit-dose package. If that drug was not entered into that patient's medication list by a pharmacist, an alert will sound, preventing the nurse from administering the wrong drug to the patient.

The unit-dose is likely stored in an automated dispensing cabinet (ADC) rather than a specific patient cassette—thus, the label will not require information such as the patient's name, prescriber's name, dispensing date, or prescription number. Since the size of the unit-dose packaging is too small to accommodate all the mandatory information on a typical label, only the following information is required:

- The drug name

- The quantity of the active ingredient

- The beyond use date (BUD)

- The lot number

- The name of the manufacturer, packager, or distributor

- Any required cautionary statements

UNIT-DOSE BEYOND USE DATE

According to the USP/NF standards, the beyond use date for unit-dose containers is no later than either of the following:

■ One year from the date the drug is repackaged, or

■ The expiration date on the manufacturer's container, whichever is earlier

CUSTOMIZED PATIENT PACKAGING FOR ADHERENCE

USP has published guidance on customized patient medication packages ("med paks"), which is found in USP 661. Instead of dispensing two or more prescribed drugs in separate containers, a pharmacist can prepare a customized med pak, with the consent of either the patient, the patient's caregiver, or the prescriber. The med pak has a series of containers, or compartments, and each compartment holds multiple doses of solid, oral drugs. Med paks make it easier to provide medications for patients on multiple doses, and are useful for increasing adherence in patients on a complicated medication regimen.

The med pak label must contain the following:

■ The name of the patient

■ A serial/prescription number for the med pak itself, and a separate serial/prescription number for each drug in the med pak

■ The name, strength, physical description, and total quantity of each drug

■ The direction for use and required cautionary statements for each drug

■ Required storage instructions

■ The name of the prescriber for each drug

■ The date of preparation of the med pak and the beyond-use date assigned to the med pak, which shall be no later than 60 days from the date that the med pak was prepared

■ The name, address, and telephone number of the pharmacy, and the pharmacy's DEA registration number, if controlled substance/s are included in the med pak

■ Any other information, statements, or warnings required for any of the drugs

■ If the patient med pak allows for the removal or separation of the intact containers, each individual container shall bear a label identifying each of the drugs inside

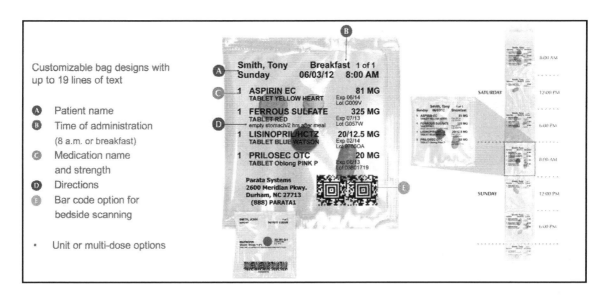

Customizable bag designs with up to 19 lines of text

A Patient name
B Time of administration (8 a.m. or breakfast)
C Medication name and strength
D Directions
E Bar code option for bedside scanning

• Unit or multi-dose options

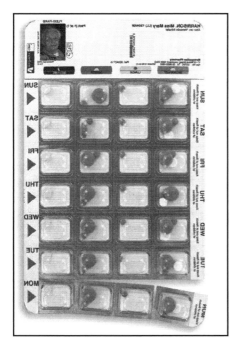

The weekly medication doses can be prepared for facility patients, or those living at home that require this assistance to help with adherence or dexterity issues.

If a drug has a patient package insert (PPI), it should be sent with the med pak. Alternatively, all the required information can be combined into a single educational insert and sent with the med pak.

In the absence of more stringent packaging requirements for any of the drugs, each container of the patient med pak shall comply with the moisture permeation requirements for a Class B single-unit or unit-dose container. Each container must be designed so that it shows evidence of having been opened or is not re-sealable.[33]

---

33   USP Chapter 17, Prescription Container Labeling (accessed 2015 Jul 30).

- In addition to any individual prescription filing requirements, a record of each patient med pak shall be made and filed. Each record should contain:

- The name and address of the patient

- The serial number of the prescription order for each of the drugs

- The name of the manufacturer or labeler and lot number for each of the drugs

- Information identifying or describing the design, characteristics, or specifications of the patient med pak sufficient to allow subsequent preparation of an identical med pak

- The date of preparation of the patient med pak and the beyond-use date that was assigned

- Any special labeling instructions

- The name or initials of the pharmacist who prepared the med pak

DRUG UTILIZATION REVIEWS

OBRA requires each state to have a drug utilization review (DUR) program in order to be reimbursed for Medicaid services. There are two types of drug utilization reviews required:

- A prospective drug utilization review; this is the evaluation of a patient's drug therapy prior to dispensing (performed by the dispensing pharmacist)

- A retrospective drug utilization review: a review of drug therapy after medication dispensing (performed by the state)

Pharmacists must perform a prospective DUR for individual Medicaid patients prior to dispensing a new prescription or refill. Most of the states have extended this requirement to include all patients. The purpose of performing a prospective DUR is to look for the following errors:

- A therapeutic duplication

- Incorrect dosing

- Incorrect treatment duration

- Contraindications to the drug

- Interactions between the drug, a disease state, or a patient allergy

- Abuse or misuse

Although pharmacy software is designed to identify drug interactions, some systems are better than others, and with all systems, the pharmacist will need to use his or her professional judgment regarding the severity of an interaction. The software can be incorrect or incomplete, with certain types of interactions missing (e.g., P-gp interactions). The pharmacist may decide to override a minor drug utilization warning, if the benefits of using the drug outweigh the risks. The pharmacist may need to recommend a dose adjustment due to an interaction. Patients may be receiving medications from more than one source, which may not show up as an interaction in the software but should be present in the medication profile if all of the drugs the patient is using have been entered. This information must be entered manually, because not all of the drugs are obtained from one pharmacy. It is common to take OTC medications and natural products, and patients can go to other pharmacies to take advantage of a less expensive generic drug cost at a different store, or they may have had a prescription transferred to take advantage of a promotional discount coupon. They may be getting some of their drugs at the veterans administration, they may be getting drugs under a patient assistance plan directly from the manufacturer, or they may be getting free drug samples from a prescriber.

The pharmacy must make a reasonable effort to update the patient profile information each time a medication is dispensed. This is why a technician or clerk at the drop off window asks the patient if there have been any changes or updates to the medications. The patient may refuse any or all of the required profile information, and if so, the pharmacy staff should document the refusal. The information required in a patient profile includes:

- Patient's name, address, telephone number

- Date of birth

- Gender

- Disease state information, drug allergies or intolerances, adverse drug reactions

- Comprehensive list of medications or devices previously dispensed

- Any relevant pharmacist comments

If an issue is present, the pharmacist must manage it according to his or her professional judgment. This will involve either contacting the prescriber for notification or clarification, and/or discussing the concern and any management necessary with the patient or caregiver.

OBRA requires the individual states to perform a system-wide retrospective DUR to analyze physician prescribing habits and assess appropriate use of certain drugs. This type of DUR is discussed in the RxPrep Course Book.

My state requires that a patient profile be kept in the pharmacy for all patients.   Yes / No

My state requires that the patient profile be kept for this time period after the last fill: _____

My state does not require patient profiles be kept for dispensing that is likely to be a one-time fill (such as a patient visiting the area who is on vacation who comes to the pharmacy with an antibiotic prescription).   Yes / No

If your state requires that the patient profile include information in addition to the items listed above, list them here:

_____

WRITTEN MATERIAL THAT IS INCLUDED AS PART OF THE PACKAGE LABELING

All information provided by the manufacturer for distribution with the drug, even if it is not physically affixed to the product, is considered part of the labeling. The drug's labeling includes:

- The drug container, such as a plastic container or bottle

- Consumer Medication Information (CMI)-not approved by the FDA

- Patient Package Inserts (PPI)-approved by the FDA

- Medication Guides (MedGuides)-approved by the FDA

- Any paperwork required as part of a REMS; see following REMS description

Consumer Medication Information

The FDA mandates that useful written patient information be provided to patients with each new prescription. The consumer medication information handouts (CMIs) are the paper leaflets of drug information that are put inside the bag, or stapled to the outside.

- The information should be simplified for patients to understand and should reflect the FDA-approved package insert.

- They should explain how to use the drug and what to expect.

- These are not reviewed or approved by the FDA.

Patient Package Inserts

In the late 1960s, the FDA required that all estrogen-containing drugs be dispensed with the FDA-approved PPI in order for the patient to be fully informed of the benefits and risks involved with the use of these drugs. Oral contraceptives for birth control were first available in 1960 and, after just 5 years, 6.5 million women were using "the pill". Initially, the estrogen content was much higher than the pills in use today. Consequently, there was a higher incidence of clotting. The FDA required the PPIs due to the lack of awareness of this risk.

The PPI must be given each time the drug is dispensed in the outpatient setting, with both the initial fill and with refills. If the PPI is not provided, it is considered misbranding. In an institutional setting such as a hospital or long-term care facility, the PPI must be provided to the patient prior to the administration of the first dose and every 30 days thereafter.

Some of the more recent drugs come with a PPI. These are voluntarily provided by the manufacturer if they feel there is important information that the patient should know about the drug. The PPIs require FDA approval. Currently, the FDA requires MedGuides to relay the risks to a patient, or, with more severe risk, a REMS program.

Medication Guides

Medication Guides (MedGuides) are FDA-approved patient handouts that come with many prescription medicines that may have a serious and significant health concern.

The FDA requires that MedGuides be issued with drugs or biologics that require certain information to prevent serious adverse events, if the patient needs to know about serious side effects or adverse events, or if adherence to specific instructions is essential to effectiveness. The manufacturer must supply the MedGuides to the dispenser by providing the physical handouts or the electronic file so the pharmacy can print them out for the patient.

Drugs that require MedGuides include all antidepressants, antipsychotics, anticonvulsants, most antiarrythmics, NSAIDs, and many others. There are over 240 medications which require MedGuides. The complete list can be found on the FDA website.

The MedGuide must be given when:

- A drug is dispensed in the outpatient setting, and the drug will be used by the patient without the supervision of a healthcare provider, with each new fill and refills

- The first time the drug is being dispensed to a healthcare provider for administration to a patient in an outpatient setting

- When the patient or their caregiver asks for it

- If the MedGuide has been revised

- If the drug is subject to a Risk Evaluation and Mitigation Strategy (REMS) that requires a MedGuide

Risk Evaluation and Mitigation Strategy

In 2007, with the enactment of the FDAAA, the FDA was given new authority to improve drug safety. One of the provisions of this act is the use of risk evaluation and mitigation strategy (REMS) that the FDA could require if a drug or biological had risks that may outweigh the benefits. The risk/benefit for any drug should always be established between the healthcare provider and the patient. If a REMS exists for a drug or drug class, the risks are considered serious and the FDA uses the REMS requirements to make sure that the risks are known and are managed adequately.

There are four parts to a REMS program:

1.   Communication plans

2.   Elements to assure safe use

3.   Implementation systems

4.   MedGuides

Key Points:

- A REMS may be required for a new drug or when safety issues arise with an existing drug.

- A REMS can be applied to an individual drug or to a drug class, such as the REMS required with long-acting opioids.

- The manufacturer (which the FDA refers to as the drug's sponsor) has to develop the REMS, and the FDA reviews it and approves it, when it is acceptable.

- Since the safety issues are different, the REMS are different, and the components will depend on the risks associated with that drug or drug class.

- The requirements include some combination of prescribing, shipping and dispensing safety requirements.

Examples of REMS Requirements

RISK	SAFETY STRATEGY
Severe infection	Patient is educated on warning signs of infection prior to prescribing.
Severe allergic reaction	Healthcare professional requires certification to administer the drug.
Liver damage	Liver function monitoring is required during use.
Severe birth defects	Negative pregnancy test required prior to dispensing each prescription.

EX. Accutane

DIETARY SUPPLEMENTS

The key differentiating factor between a drug and a dietary supplement is the health claim of the product. When a claim is made that the product cures, prevents, corrects or treats a disease or condition the product is considered a drug. In contrast, the manufacturer of a dietary supplement is permitted to claim that a supplement addresses a nutrient deficiency, supports health or is linked to body functions. The product cannot claim that it cures, treats, corrects or prevents or other terms that suggest treatment or prevention of a disease. Naming a dietary supplement CarpalHealth or CircuCure implies that it can treat carpal tunnel or improve your circulation; these are disease claims and are not acceptable for dietary supplements. "Supports intestinal health" is acceptable but "effective relief for heartburn" is not. "Relax and sleep" is acceptable but "cures insomnia" is not. The Supplement Facts box is required on all dietary supplements.

The label uses the acceptable wording "helps support gastrointestinal health" and does not claim to prevent, treat or cure an illness.

→ not for OTC drugs (dietary suppl)

The product must include a disclaimer that the FDA has not evaluated the claim and must have supporting research to back up any claims made in advertising or in the package labeling.

There are requirements for supplements under the DSHEA regulations that must be met for identity, purity, quality, strength and composition. The manufacturer can be held liable if there are possible safety concerns. If a problem exists with a supplement it is reported by the consumer or by the manufacturer through the FDA's Safety Reporting Portal (SRP), an online system similar to MedWatch. The FDA is responsible for taking action if there are any safety concerns, including adulteration or misbranding.

Supplement Facts
Serving Size 1 Tablet

	Amount Per Serving	% Daily Value
Vitamin A (as retinyl acetate and 50% as beta-carotene)	5000 IU	100%
Vitamin C (as ascorbic acid)	60 mg	100%
Vitamin D (as cholecalciferol)	400 IU	100%
Vitamin E (as di-alpha tocopheryl acetate)	30 IU	100%
Thiamin (as thiamin mononitrate)	1.5 mg	100%
Riboflavin	1.7 mg	100%
Niacin (as niacinamide)	20 mg	100%
Vitamin B_6 (as pyridoxine hydrochloride)	2.0 mg	100%
Folate (as folic acid)	400 mcg	100%
Vitamin B_{12} (as cyanocobalamin)	6 mcg	100%
Biotin	30 mcg	10%
Pantothenic Acid (as calcium pantothenate)	10 mg	100%

Other ingredients: Gelatin, lactose, magnesium stearate, microcrystalline cellulose, FD&C Yellow No. 6, propylene glycol, propylparaben, and sodium benzoate.

Dietary Supplement Facts Box

Dietary Supplement Labels

Information that must be on a dietary supplement label includes a descriptive name of the product, the wording "supplement" or "dietary supplement", the name and address of the manufacturer, packer or distributor, a complete list of ingredients and the net contents, which is the amount in the container. Each dietary supplement (with the exception of some small volume products or those produced by eligible small businesses) must include the "Supplement Facts" box on the label.

Dietary Supplements Must Follow Current Good Manufacturing Practices

In 2007 the FDA published regulations for current good manufacturing practices (CGMPs) that supplement manufacturers must meet. These are described further. The manufacturer is responsible for quality control procedures, designing and constructing the manufacturing plants, and testing ingredients and the finished product. Requirements for packaging, labeling, storage, recordkeeping and handling consumer product complaints are included.

PATIENT IDENTIFICATION PRIOR TO DISPENSING OR ADMINISTERING PRESCRIPTION DRUGS

Some states require the pharmacy staff to verify the patient's identity in order to prevent drug diversion and reduce medication errors. There is presently no federal law requiring patients to provide identification prior to receiving prescriptions. In the community setting, the most commonly used identifiers are the patient's name and date of birth. If the patient has a common name, the home address can be requested for additional verification. Some states require patient identification for all prescriptions in the community setting while other states require identification only for controlled substances.

 *First/Last name; MM/DD*

Is patient identification required in your state in order to dispense all drugs in the community pharmacy setting? (Yes) / No   *ID for CS*

Is patient identification required in your state for controlled substance dispensing only? Yes / No

In order to reduce errors, institutional settings certified by The Joint Commission require healthcare providers to verify two patient identifiers prior to administering a drug or performing a procedure.[34] The identifiers must be patient-specific, therefore identifiers that can be used for many patients are not acceptable (such as the prescriber's name, or the patient's city or zip code). In an institution setting such as a hospital, the medical record number (usually located on the patient's wrist band) and the patient's name or date of birth are commonly used.[35]

PATIENT COUNSELING

Pursuant to OBRA 90, pharmacists must offer oral consultation before dispensing prescriptions to Medicaid patients. The majority of states have made the offer to counsel a mandatory requirement for all patients. Some state laws only mandate the offer to counsel for new prescriptions, while other states mandate the offer to counsel for refills as well. Although the offer to counsel must be made, the patient or patient's caregiver may refuse counseling.

Counseling Face-to-Face

The pharmacist provides patient counseling in an area suitable for confidential patient consultation to protect the patient's privacy, including the protected health information. Depending on individual state requirements, the patient consultation may be initiated by the pharmacist or by other pharmacy personnel. For example, some states allow any personnel to ask the patient "would you like to be counseled by the pharmacist?" whereas other states mandate that the pharmacist must personally ask

the patient if he or she would like to be counseled. In all states, the pharmacist must provide the actual counseling. It is up to the pharmacist's judgment to decide which information should be discussed with the patient during counseling. Due to time limitations, pharmacists may discuss select information.

34   The Joint Commission's National Patient Safety Goal NPSG 01.01.01.
35   http://www.cms.gov/Medicare-Medicaid-Coordination/Fraud-Prevention/Medicaid-Integrity-Education/Provider-Education-Toolkits/Downloads/drugdiversion-patientcounseling-111414.pdf (accessed 2015 Jul 15).

Patient counseling can include:

- Name and description of drug

- Route of administration

- Dosage form

- Dose

- Duration of therapy

- How to prepare drug for administration

- Techniques for self-monitoring

- Common and/or severe adverse drug reactions or interactions

- What to do if a dose is missed

- Prescription refill information

- Importance of compliance

- Storage

Counseling When the Patient is Not Present

Many states still require an "offer" of counseling when prescriptions are delivered to home or work, or sent through the mail or by a delivery service. An acceptable method is to provide the pharmacy business hours and a toll-free phone number on the printed drug information or container label. Some states require mail-order pharmacies to be open for a minimum number of hours and days per week to receive patient calls.

mail Order pharmacy

1) The written offer to counsel must be included with the mailed RX.

2) Pharmacy's ph. number must be included.

3) Try to contact pt within 48hrs since drug was mailed.

My state requires the pharmacy's hours and a toll-free number to be listed on the prescription container labeling.   Yes / No

My state requires mail-order pharmacies to be open for a defined number of days and hours per week. Yes / No

List any other counseling requirements for medications delivered to the patient or sent by mail:

_____

_____

_____

Counseling the Limited-English Proficient Patient

Depending on local and regional demographics, pharmacies may interact with patients with limited grasp of the English language. The largest number of limited-English proficient (LEP) patients who speak Spanish, Chinese, Korean, Vietnamese, or Tagalog are located in New York, California, Texas and Florida. All patients in the United States need to know how to safely use their medication. In states with large immigrant populations, the state board may have specific protocols and requirements for communicating with LEP patients. This may include the use of a language translator to assist with patient counseling.

My state does/does not require pharmacies to provide translation services to LEP patients.

If yes, list the acceptable methods, if specified:

_____

Exemptions for Patient Counseling

Many states will not require pharmacists to counsel on patients receiving institutional care, such as in a hospital. It is presumed that the healthcare provider or related staff taking care of the patient will provide any necessary drug information. Some hospitals will send pharmacists to the floor to review the drugs being given or to provide counseling when the patient is ready to be discharged, which is called "discharge counseling".

Another exception to providing patient counseling is when the patient or caregiver has been offered counseling, and the offer has been refused.

Counseling Requirements by State

A summary of counseling requirements is provided by CMS' Position Paper on Patient Counseling Requirements, and can be accessed on the CMS page referenced in the footnote. In different states, different personnel are permitted to make the offer to counsel. The required content of the counseling is reviewed in the pharmacy practice section.[36]

Table 1. State Compliance Requirements and Patient Counseling Documentation Requirements by State

State	Require oral counseling in certain situations or an "offer to counsel"	Documentation of "offer to counsel" required by State	Documentation of patient's refusal for counseling	Counsel new prescriptions and refills	Process for counseling when patient is not in the pharmacy	Discuss with patient prior to generic substitution	Require distribution of written materials
Alabama	Y	Y	N	N	N	N	Y
Alaska	Y	N	N	N	Y	Y	N
Arizona	Y	Y	Y	N	Y	Y	Y
Arkansas	Y	N	N	N	Y	Y	N
California	Y	Y	N	N	Y	Y	Y
Colorado	Y	Y	Y	N	N	Y	Y
Connecticut	Y	Y	Y	Y	N	Y	N
Delaware	Y	Y	Y	N	Y	Y	Y
District of Columbia	Y	Y	Y	N	Y	N	Y
Florida	Y	Y	N	Y	Y	Y	Y
Georgia	Y	N	N	Y	Y	N	N
Hawaii	N	Y	N	N	N	Y	Y
Idaho	Y	Y	N	Y	N	N	N
Illinois	Y	Y	Y	Y	N	N	N
Indiana	Y	Y	N	Y	Y	N	Y
Iowa	Y	Y	Y	N	N	N	N
Kansas	Y	Y	N	N	N	Y	N
Kentucky	Y	Y	Y	N	N	N	Y
Louisiana	N	N	N	N	N	N	N
Maine	Y	Y	Y	N	Y	Y	Y
Maryland	Y	N	N	N	N	Y	Y
Massachusetts	Y	Y	Y	N	Y	N	N
Michigan	Y	Y	N	N	Y	Y	N
Minnesota	Y	Y	N	N	Y	Y	Y
Mississippi	Y	Y	N	Y	Y	Y	N
Missouri	Y	N	N	Y	Y	N	Y
Montana	Y	Y	Y	N	N	N	N
Nebraska	Y	Y	Y	Y	N	Y	N
Nevada	Y	Y	N	N	Y	Y	N
New Hampshire	Y	Y	N	N	Y	Y	Y
New Jersey	Y	Y	Y	N	Y	N	N
New Mexico	Y	Y	N	N	Y	N	Y
New York	Y	Y	Y	N	Y	Y	Y
North Carolina	Y	Y	N	N	Y	N	N

36   http://www.cms.gov/Medicare-Medicaid-Coordination/Fraud-Prevention/Medicaid-Integrity-Education/Provider-Education-Toolkits/Downloads/drugdiversion-patientcounseling-111414.pdf (accessed 2015 Aug 5).

State	Require oral counseling in certain situations or an "offer to counsel"	Documentation of "offer to counsel" required by State	Documentation of patient's refusal for counseling	Counsel new prescriptions and refills	Process for counseling when patient is not in the pharmacy	Discuss with patient prior to generic substitution	Require distribution of written materials
North Dakota	Y	N	N	Y	Y	Y	Y
Ohio	Y	Y	Y	Y	Y	N	N
Oklahoma	Y	Y	N	N	Y	N	N
Oregon	Y	N	Y	N	Y	Y	N
Pennsylvania	Y	Y	Y	N	Y	Y	Y
Rhode Island	Y	Y	Y	N	N	Y	N
South Carolina	Y	Y	N	N	N	Y	N
South Dakota	Y	N	Y	N	Y	N	Y
Tennessee	Y	Y	N	N	Y	N	N
Texas	Y	Y	Y	N	Y	Y	Y
Utah	Y	Y	Y	N	Y	Y	N
Vermont	N	Y	Y	Y	N	N	N
Virginia	Y	Y	Y	N	Y	Y	Y
Washington	Y	N	N	Y	Y	N	Y
West Virginia	Y	Y	Y	N	N	Y	N
Wisconsin	Y	N	N	Y	Y	N	N
Wyoming	Y	Y	Y	N	N	N	N
Total number of States with requirement	48	40	25	14	33	28	24

HEALTH INSURANCE PORTABILITY AND ACCOUNTABILITY ACT

The Health Insurance Portability and Accountability Act (HIPAA) protects the privacy of the patient's health information, outlines how it can be shared, and provides the patient the right to access their own information. HIPAA also involves insurance portability, which allows individuals to keep their insurance if transitioning from one job to another.

Pharmacists are more concerned with protecting the privacy of the patient health information. All healthcare professionals who have access to confidential patient information must have documented HIPAA training. Violation of HIPAA, either inadvertently or deliberately, can result in fines and imprisonment. An individual at each facility must be designated to enforce the privacy policy.

Examples of privacy abuse include:

■ Labels with identifiers sent to shredding (recycling) company

■ Pharmacy employees snooping around in celebrity patient records

■ Pictures or information about patients posted on social media sites

The information covered under HIPAA is called protected health information (PHI) and includes private information in electronic, verbal, or written form. According to HIPAA, PHI includes:

■ The patient's past, present, or future physical or mental health or condition (e.g., the medical record)

■ The healthcare provided to the patient (e.g., laboratory tests, surgery)

■ The past, present, or future payment for providing healthcare to the patient, which can identify the patient. (e.g., hospital bills)

Protected health information includes many common identifiers, such as the name, address, birth date and social security number when they can be associated with the health information listed above. If the identifying information is not related to health information, then it is not considered PHI. For example, names, residential addresses, or phone numbers listed in a public directory such as a phone book would not be PHI because there is no health data associated with it.

The healthcare facility or pharmacy must ensure that any patient information is secure and not available to viewers who do not require the access. Healthcare providers must be mindful of the following:

■ Avoid discussing patient care in elevators

■ Shred all documents prior to disposal

■ Cover patient identifiers on prescription bottles and bags prior and during dispensing

■ Close patient records on computer screens when not in use and logout of the system

Incidental disclosures are not a violation, such as calling out a patient's name in a waiting room, discussing a patient's care during medical rounds, or using patient sign-in sheets in waiting rooms.

The "minimum necessary" information required for the job is what should be shared. This becomes an issue for pharmacists when the insurer may not wish to pay without additional information, which the pharmacist may not think is required. Minimum necessary is also designed to encourage the pharmacy or practice site to evaluate who should be accessing patient records. If support staff do not need patient medical records to do their jobs, they should not have access. A pharmacy student accessing a relative's medical records at a hospital during their intern experience (when they are not involved with the relative's medical care at the facility) would constitute a privacy violation.

It is permissible to share PHI with:

- The patient

- Other healthcare providers providing care to the patient

- Persons requiring the information for treatment, payment, or operational purposes

- Others, when authorized by the patient

- A limited data set can be provided for research, public health or institutional operations

- Law enforcement, the DEA, the FDA, medical board inspectors, pharmacy board inspectors (for a public health purpose or drug abuse concern)

Pharmacists may leave voicemails regarding medications on patients' home machines, discuss care with patients' family members or caregivers, and provide written material. Prescriptions can be picked up by family or friends unless the pharmacist has reason to believe that this would be against the wishes of the patient.

If the release of patient health information is not for purposes of treatment, payment, or operations, the pharmacist must receive the patient's written authorization. This authorization must include whom the information will be shared with, the purpose, the expiration date, and the patient's signature. If the patient is requesting the release, a written authorization is not necessary according to HIPAA, but some facilities will require it.

The Notice of Privacy Practices

HIPAA requires a site-specific notice on the policies in place to protect patient information and to whom the information can be shared. This should be in simple language, and state the patient's rights to their own information and be specific that any release beyond that which is stated in the policy will require the patient's approval. It should list the contact for Department of Health & Human Services if the patient wishes to file a complaint, along with the contact for a person within the pharmacy if the patient wishes to discuss privacy concerns.

The privacy notice must be given to the patient on the first day that service is provided. The pharmacy must make a good faith effort to obtain the patient's written acknowledgement of the receipt of the notice. There is no requirement for future signatures, although some workplaces require the patient to resign on an annual basis. The pharmacy can still provide services if the patient refuses to sign. This written acknowledgement must be separate from other signatures. This means that one signature cannot be used to both acknowledge receipt of the HIPAA privacy notice, and to acknowledge another item, such as refusing the right to counsel. The signature for HIPAA must be separate. The HIPAA privacy notice should also be placed in a prominent location within the pharmacy and on the pharmacy's website. The patient has a right to request all of their privacy disclosures for the past 6 years; thus, the HIPAA signed privacy disclosure forms must be kept for 6 years.

Provide HIPPA:
- When the privacy practice is updated
- At the request of the patient.

DRUG SUBSTITUTION OR SELECTION

Generic Drug Substitution

Every state has a generic drug substitution law, which permits or mandates the pharmacist to substitute a brand name drug with a generic drug. The purpose is to provide the patient with a lower cost drug, while still providing the same therapeutic benefit. Drug substitution laws vary by state. Most state laws permit pharmacists to substitute generic, therapeutically-equivalent drugs for the branded drug using the FDA's *Orange Book: Approved Drug Products with Therapeutic Equivalence Evaluations*, unless the prescriber and/or patient has requested otherwise. If a drug is listed as a generic equivalent in the *Orange Book*, it means that the generic has demonstrated pharmaceutical equivalence and bioequivalence (pharmaceutical equivalence and bioequivalence are further defined in the next section). Not all states reference the *Orange Book;* for example, in Georgia, "A pharmacist may substitute a drug with the same generic name in the same strength, quantity, dose, and dosage form as the prescribed brand name drug product which is, in the pharmacist's reasonable professional opinion, pharmaceutically equivalent." (Georgia Code, Title 26, Chapter 4, Article 5, 2014).

When a prescriber writes the brand name of a drug on a prescription, the pharmacist may substitute with a generic as long as the prescriber has not indicated otherwise. If the prescriber writes or checks off a box with his/her initials that states DO NOT SUBSTITUTE, no substitution can be made. Some state laws permit the pharmacist to decide whether or not to make a generic substitution; this is called a permissive drug product selection law. Other states make it mandatory to make a generic substitution unless the patient or prescriber has noted otherwise; this is called a mandatory drug product selection law.

It is considered misbranding if the pharmacist labeled a generic drug as the brand drug, or vice versa. This practice may be done because the pharmacist is attempting to increase profits by billing insurance for the more expensive brand name drug but dispensing a lower cost generic drug.

My state permits generic substitution according to the *Orange Book,* unless certain action/s have been taken by the prescriber and/or patient. Yes / No

If yes, list the actions that must be taken to prevent generic interchange:

DAW
_____

My state permits generic substitution according to requirements other than the *Orange Book.* Yes / No

If yes, list the requirements and the actions a prescriber and/or patient can take to block the substitution:

_____

Using the Orange Book

The Food and Drug Administration publishes and frequently updates the *Approved Drug Products with Therapeutic Equivalence Evaluations* (commonly known as the *Orange Book*), which serves as a guide for therapeutically equivalent drugs.

The *Orange Book* uses a two-letter code system. If the first letter is "A", it is therapeutically equivalent to the brand name drug, also called the "reference listed drug (RLD)" since the "brand name" drug was on the market first and is used as a reference to compare all the other generics to. If the first letter is "B", then it is not considered therapeutically equivalent. The second letter tells you what kind of formulation the drug is.

In some instances, (e.g., levothyroxine) a number is added to the end of the two letters to make a 3-character code (AB1, AB2, AB3, etc.) Three-character codes are assigned when more than one RLD of the same strength has been designated under the same heading. With levothyroxine, a generic dosage that has a 3-character code can be used to substitute for 3 different branded drugs with the same dose.

The Electronic *Orange Book* (EOB) can be accessed on the FDA website at http://www.accessdata.fda.gov/scripts/cder/ob/default.cfm.

A or AB rated only

N021402	AB1,AB2	No	LEVOTHYROXINE SODIUM	TABLET; ORAL	0.2MG **See current Annual Edition, 1.8 Description of Special Situations, Levothyroxine Sodium	SYNTHROID	ABBVIE
N021402	AB1,AB2	Yes	LEVOTHYROXINE SODIUM	TABLET; ORAL	0.3MG **See current Annual Edition, 1.8 Description of Special Situations, Levothyroxine Sodium	SYNTHROID	ABBVIE
N021210	AB1,AB2,AB3	No	LEVOTHYROXINE SODIUM	TABLET; ORAL	0.025MG **See current Annual Edition, 1.8 Description of Special Situations, Levothyroxine Sodium	UNITHROID	STEVENS ,
N021210	AB1,AB2,AB3	No	LEVOTHYROXINE SODIUM	TABLET; ORAL	0.05MG **See current Annual Edition, 1.8 Description of Special Situations, Levothyroxine Sodium	UNITHROID	STEVENS ,

Orange book listing for some of the levothyroxine oral tablets.

Narrow Therapeutic Index Drug Substitution

Narrow therapeutic index (NTI) drugs are defined as drugs where small differences in dose or blood concentration could cause treatment failure or toxicity. NTI drugs have very small differences between the subtherapeutic dose, the therapeutic dose, and the toxic dose. Even small differences in bioavailability between generic drugs can cause a significant difference in serum drug concentration. Examples of NTI drugs include lithium, digoxin and warfarin. Each of these drugs requires close monitoring.

Several states (Florida, Idaho, Kentucky, Maine, Minnesota, North Carolina, Pennsylvania, Rhode Island and Hawaii) do not permit substitution of NTI drugs and will define an NTI list that could include a few or up to a dozen different NTI drugs. This is commonly referred to as a negative formulary. In these states, the NTI drug must be dispensed with the same formulation from the same manufacturer as was previously filled to provide therapeutic consistency for the patient, unless the prescriber and/or the patient have been notified and consents to the change.

My state permits substitution of NTI drugs unless this action/s has been taken by the prescriber and/or patient. Yes / No

_____

My state does not routinely permit the pharmacist to substitute an NTI drug. Yes / No

NTI drugs that cannot be substituted in my state include:

_____

Biologics and Biosimilars

Biologics are discussed under the Biologics Price Competition and Innovation Act (BPCI) of 2000. Biologics are manufactured from living organisms by programming cell lines to produce the desired therapeutic substances. They are complex, large molecules. True generics for biologics are not possible according to the conventional definition, therefore the term biosimilar is used instead. Common biologics in use today include human growth hormone, injectable treatments for arthritis and psoriasis, among others. The first biosimilar was approved in 2014.

Drug Formularies

A formulary is a preferred drug list that the institution, healthcare plan, or pharmacy benefit manager (PBM) has chosen for their patients or members. The formulary should include the safest and effective drugs, be in accord with current clinical guidelines, and take into consideration the cost-effectiveness of the drug.

In hospitals, prescribers usually select drugs available on the institution's formulary. Formularies used in institutions such as hospitals are open formularies, which means that any drug on the formulary can be chosen without a variable cost structure.

Healthcare plans have formularies to outline which drugs will be covered in the outpatient or retail setting. Patients can refer to these formularies to be aware of different tiers and co-pays. The typical formulary for outpatient use has 3, 4, or 5 tiers. The lower tier level has a lower co-pay. A co-pay is the out-of-pocket expense that the patient is responsible for in order to receive healthcare related services such as prescriber visits and prescription drugs. Specialty drugs, which are primarily biologics, can be included at a higher tier. Specialty drugs, most often, are obtained from a specialty pharmacy. The specialty pharmacy will be connected to or contracted with the insurance company or PBM.

A pharmacy benefit manager, as the name implies, manages the pharmacy "benefit" for a healthcare system or as a third-party payer for groups that contract with the PBM to manage all aspects of drug use. For example, *Express Scripts*, one of the larger PBMs, is contracted by many insurance companies and large employers to manage the client's drug benefit. The management includes selecting drugs to include on the formulary, formulary maintenance, insurance billing, pharmacy central filling and prescription delivery (mail order), community pharmacy payment

Copay/ coinsurance tier**	Type of drug
Tier 1	Covered generic drugs***
Tier 2	Covered preferred brand-name drugs
Tier 3	Covered non-preferred generic or brand-name drugs***

Usual Drugs by Tier

processing, and software systems that enable the individual patients to manage their benefit online and for the clients to manage their services and costs.

The formulary system usually includes prescribing guidelines and other clinical decision making tools to help prescribers select the preferred drugs. An online system can be designed so that only preferred drugs can be chosen, unless some type of exception has been authorized. Some systems incorporate the laboratory values to assist with drug selection. For example, if lisinopril is chosen, the system would check or make visible the potassium level and the renal function.

If a drug has a history of unsafe use, it may be withdrawn from the formulary. If there are "look-alike, sound-alike" drugs, the P&T committee (described below) may remove one of them to avoid mix-ups. If multiple drugs have similar risk-benefit profiles, it is likely the least expensive drug will be included and the pricier drug will not. Or, if one agent has safety risks but is effective in refractory cases, it can be given "restricted use" status and can be used only if the patient has failed the first-line agents, or perhaps can only be selected by specialists in that area of medicine.

When similar drugs exist in a class, a competitive bidding process is used. For example, if a P&T committee wishes to select a prostaglandin analogue for glaucoma, and there are five equally safe and effective agents on the market, the committee can choose the least expensive option available, and may have a second agent on tier 2 that was also chosen based on competitive bidding. In many cases, if the patient chooses to use a drug from the most expensive tier, the patient is covering most of the cost of the drug. These are occasionally drugs that would not otherwise be on the formulary due to the cost involved and the availability of less expensive options. Yet, the patient or prescriber wants it on the formulary, so it is added as a high-tier agent and the costs are passed along to the patient.

Pharmacy & Therapeutics Committee

The P&T committee is responsible for managing the formulary and all aspects of drug use in a healthcare system, which could be a small hospital or a large PBM. The P&T members would include physicians, pharmacists, nurse/s, administrator/s, quality improvement manager/s and the medication safety officer. The primary responsibilities of the P&T committee are to create and update the formulary (a continual process as drugs change), conduct medication (or drug) use evaluation (MUE/DUE), have responsibility for adverse drug event monitoring and reporting, and conduct medication error safety initiatives (which will involve the medication safety officer) and develop the clinical care plans and protocols. This includes the development of protocols to guide the use of high-alert drugs, which have a high risk of causing patient harm when used incorrectly.

Formulary members who serve on the P&T committee

Hospital pharmacists rely on guidance from the American Society of Hospital Pharmacists (ASHP), the Joint Commission, the Institute of Safe Medication Practices (ISMP) and select professional organizations for best practices in hospitals, such as high-alert drug protocol development, management of blood products, quality assurance for sterile compounding, therapeutic interchange, and many other areas related to the practice of hospital pharmacy.

Therapeutic Equivalence/Therapeutic Interchange

Therapeutic equivalents are drug products with different chemical structures that are of the same pharmacological class, and usually can be expected to have similar outcomes and adverse reaction profiles when administered in therapeutically equivalent doses.

Therapeutic equivalence in a community setting usually means something different than therapeutic equivalence in a hospital setting. The community pharmacist is looking for a generic substitution for a branded drug, while the hospital pharmacist is looking for a different drug in the same pharmacological class, in an equivalent dose. For example, if branded rosuvastatin (*Crestor*) is not on the formulary, but the generic drugs atorvastatin and simvastatin are on the formulary, the hospital pharmacist will choose the therapeutically equivalent dose of one of the two available statins when *Crestor* has been ordered. The formulation may be switched. For example, if a prescriber orders intravenous levofloxacin for a patient who is consuming a normal diet and has a mild-moderate infection, the formulation is likely to be interchanged to oral levofloxacin. Converting to oral administration reduces the drug cost, the pharmacy preparation time, the nursing time to hang the IV bag, and will reduce infection risk by maintaining an intact skin barrier.

The pharmacist who made the "interchange" of one drug to another will not need to discuss the change with the prescriber as long as the drugs are able to be exchanged under the hospital's "therapeutic interchange" protocol, which is followed in order to reduce drug costs and inpatient days. The therapeutic interchange protocol is a collaboration between pharmacists and physicians in an institution (e.g., hospitals, nursing facilities or transitional care settings). Therapeutic interchange has become much more important in recent years because of the increase in the number of similar drugs in the same class. The P&T committee will determine the drugs included in the institution's therapeutic interchange protocol. Antacids, quinolones, potassium supplements, cephalosporins, statins, insulins and laxatives are commonly interchanged in this manner.

PHARMACY COMPOUNDING

Traditional Compounding and Section 503A

In November 2013, under section 503A of the Drug Quality and Security Act (DQSA), drug products prepared using traditional compounding methods were given three exemptions from requirements that apply to prescription drugs:

- Compliance with current good manufacturing practices (CGMP)

- Labeling with adequate directions for use

- The need to obtain FDA approval for the new drug product

Traditional compounding must be performed by a licensed pharmacist (or in some cases, by a physician), and be based on a prescription that has been written for an individual patient. Traditional compounding enables the pharmacist to prepare a drug formulation to fit the unique needs of an individual patient. There are valid reasons why this type of compounding may be required:

- If a drug exists only in a tablet or capsule and the patient has difficulty swallowing hard formulations

- In shortages; for example, if a drug typically comes in a suspension for children's use but only the capsule formulation is available, a pharmacist may compound the capsule contents into a suspension[37]

- To create a dose or concentration that is not commercially available

- To add flavoring for palatability

- To exclude inactive ingredients (excipients) that an individual patient has an allergy or sensitivity to, such as wheat, lactose or a certain preservative

Section 503A also permits the pharmacist to prepare small batches of a compounded preparation in advance if the dispensing history of the store supports the need. The primary reason for this allowance is convenience; it takes time to set up ingredients and equipment, prepare the product, document the preparation, and clean the area. If a pharmacist in a medical building prepares 3-4 prescriptions of the same strength of a progesterone cream each day, the pharmacy can prepare a few days' worth of the cream so it is ready when the prescriptions are received. Federal law does not define an exact amount of compounded drug that can be prepared in advance, but some states define a set number of days (such as 3 days). These preparations will need to be labeled with the appropriate beyond use date (BUD).

37 For example, in the 2009-2010 H1N1 influenza pandemic, there was a shortage of liquid Tamiflu. Pharmacists in almost every state were able to compound the capsules into flavored suspensions in order to fill prescriptions written for young children.

Not applicable to animal compounding drugs pharmacy

Outsourcing Facilities and Section 503B

In 2012, manufacturing under the guise of compounding led to 698 fungal infections in 19 states, with some fatalities, at the infamous (and since shut down) New England Compounding Center (NECC) in Massachusetts. The pharmacists at NECC prepared vials of methylprednisolone injections in bulk in order to capitalize on a shortage. Some of the lots were contaminated due to a lack of aseptic technique and product quality testing. These were sent all over the country. Pharmacists involved with NECC have been charged with murder, racketeering and mail fraud due to the gross negligence involved with these preparations. The reason that NECC was able to market the methylprednisolone injections was because the drug was in short supply. This is not the purpose for traditional compounding, which is not intended to replace commercially available drugs. Yet, shortages exist commonly and in some cases a pharmacy can compound a preparation to meet the need for the drug. In order to respond to this need, section 503B was added to the DQSA, which permits pharmacies to register with the FDA as an "outsourcing facility" in order to bulk compound and distribute drugs across state lines if the following requirements are met:

- The drugs must be compounded in compliance with CGMPs

- The facility pays a fee to the FDA, and is subject to FDA inspection

- The preparations must be made by or under the supervision of a licensed pharmacist

- The facility must meet recordkeeping requirements, including the source of the ingredients, sterility data, and the adverse event history

If the requirements under section 503B had been in place prior to the fiasco at NECC, (and if they had registered as an outsourcing facility and thus were adhering to CGMPs) it is likely that the situation would have been avoided. The current goal is to prevent a repeat of this type of practice while still providing a way to obtain some of the drugs in short supply.

Compounding is also used for research or teaching purposes and in chemical analysis; these preparations are not sold or dispensed at pharmacies.

Compounding Versus Manufacturing

Manufacturing involves the development and production of licensed drugs, which are produced in bulk for groups of patients rather than for an individual patient. Outsourcing facility pharmacies can bulk-compound—this is an explicit exception provided under 503B.

- Manufacturing is regulated by the FDA; compounding is regulated by state boards except for the requirements for outsourcing facilities[38]

- Manufacturing requires CGMPs; compounding does not, unless it is an outsourcing facility

38 http://www.fda.gov/downloads/drugs/guidancecomplianceregulatoryinformation/guidances/ucm377051.pdf (accessed 2015 Jul 25).

■ Manufacturing does not require a prescription; individual compounding is done by prescription for a specific patient

■ Manufactured drugs have NDC numbers; compounded drugs do not

■ Outsourcing facilities require a separate license, must register with the FDA, but are not registered as drug manufacturers, and the agency does not approve their prescriptions before marketing, nor automatically receive adverse events reports

My state has additional requirements for compounding that go beyond federal requirements. Yes / No

If yes, list the additional compounding requirements: _____

_____

My state permits drugs that were compounded in another state to be sent to patients in my state. Yes / No

If yes, list the requirements that must be met (such as any required inspections, required permits and fees):

_____

Non-Sterile Compounding

Community pharmacies regularly perform non-sterile compounding on a routine basis. Some states define mixing water with powder for a suspension as compounding. Other states do not refer to this process as compounding; it is simply referred to as reconstitution. The non-sterile compounding chapter in the RxPrep Course book describes commonly used compounding equipment (balances, spatulas, etc.), preparations (suspensions, emulsions, etc.) and terminology (levigation, trituration, etc.).

The compounding master formula, record log and label requirements are provided in detail in USP Chapter 795 in the Revision Bulletin of January 2014.[39]

Sterile Compounding

The most common type of sterile compounding is preparing IV medications in a hospital setting. If the medication is not prepared in an aseptic manner and becomes contaminated, the pathogen (which will be injected directly into the patient's blood stream) could cause infection. This is what caused the large number of infections and fatalities with the NECC fiasco.

---

39   USP Chapter 795, Revision Bulletin of January 2014, available at www.usp.org

Sterile compounding is required for injections, inhalations, wound and cavity irrigation baths, eye drops and eye ointments. Water used in a sterile preparation must be sterile water for injection, or bacteriostatic water for injection. Sterile compounding requires personnel trained and evaluated at least annually for competency in aseptic techniques, environmental control, quality assurance testing and end-product evaluation and sterility testing. If the product is an injectable, the certified sterile compounding environment must be either an ISO class 5 (class 100) laminar air flow hood within an ISO class 7 (class 10,000) clean room (with positive air pressure differential relative to adjacent areas) or an ISO class 5 (class 100) clean room with positive air pressure differential relative to adjacent areas or a barrier isolator that provides an ISO class 5 (class 100) environment.[40]

Clean room garb (low-shedding coverall, head cover, face mask and shoe covers) is required and should be put on and taken off outside the designated area. Hand, finger and wrist jewelry is not allowed. Head and facial hair have to be out of the way (tied up) and covered. Cytotoxic agents require specialized gowns, gloves, masks and product labeling.

Master Formulation Record

The formulation record is the formula or "recipe" book that the pharmacy uses to prepare compounded products. This is the "how-to" instructions for the compounded products made at that pharmacy. Some of the formulas may be based on the store's past experience and others will come from professional compounding compendia.

The formulation record must be complete enough to enable any competent staff member to follow the instructions and replicate the product. The formulation record should include:

■ The official or assigned name, strength, and dosage form of the preparation

■ The calculations needed to determine and verify the quantities of the components and the doses of the active pharmaceutical ingredients (APIs)

■ A description of all ingredients and their quantities

■ Compatibility, stability and storage information, including references when available

■ Equipment needed to prepare the preparation

40   USP Chapter 797, Sterile Compounding, available at www.usp.org

- Appropriate mixing instructions that should include:

  - ❑ Order of mixing

  - ❑ Mixing temperatures or other environmental controls

  - ❑ Duration of mixing

The Compounding Record or Log Book

The compounding record book is used to document individual products prepared and should include:

- Official or assigned name

- Strength and dosage of the preparation

- Master Formulation Record reference for the preparation

- Names and quantities of all components

- Sources, lot numbers, and expiration dates of all components

- Total quantity compounded

- Name of the person who prepared the preparation

- Name of the person who performed the quality control procedures

- Name of the compounding pharmacist who approved the preparation

- Date of preparation

- Assigned control or prescription number

- Assigned BUD

- Duplicate container label that is placed in the log book

- Description of final preparation

- Results of quality control procedures (e.g., weight range of filled capsules, pH of aqueous liquids)

- Documentation of any quality control issues and any adverse reactions or preparation problems reported by the patient or caregiver

Compounded Product Labels

The label on the container must include:

- Generic name

- Quantity or concentration of each active ingredient (for capsules include the mcg or mg/capsule)

- Beyond use date

- Storage conditions

- The prescription or control number, whichever is applicable

- Container used in dispensing

- Any required auxiliary labels (such as "Shake Well" for emulsions and suspensions, "Keep Refrigerated", "External Use Only")

- The label should include the statement or similar "This is a compounded preparation"

- Packaging and storage requirements

Staff Training Requirements for Compounding

All staff require on-going, periodic training for the type of compounding conducted. The staff need to be evaluated at least annually. During the training session, the steps are demonstrated to the staff that will be making preparations. The staff must be able to demonstrate the steps back, without instruction. All training and evaluation results must be documented. Steps in the training procedure should include:

- Knowledge of the USP Chapter on Non-Sterile and/or Sterile Compounding and other relevant publications

- All procedures used

- Hazardous compound training

The compounding pharmacist who has signed off on the product is responsible for the finished preparation.

Beyond Use Dating and Expiration Dates for Compounded Products

The USP emphasizes that beyond use date (BUD) should be applied conservatively. The table that follows includes maximum use dates for non-sterile products that are used in the absence of stability testing. If an expiration date of any of the active pharmaceutical ingredients (API) is sooner than the BUD, the earlier expiration date is used. If drug-specific stability data is available, it should be used to make the BUD determination.

The storage must be considered; products kept in a refrigerator will usually be stable for longer periods than products left at room temperature since heat speeds up chemical reactions that can degrade the substance. The container can be chosen to block out light and moisture. Light and humidity exposure contributes to degradation. Preservatives may be required to block microbial contamination. The preservatives are required in sterile formulations that contain more than one dose.[41]

FORMULATION	BEYOND USE DATE
Nonaqueous Formulations (lotions, creams, ointments, etc.)	The BUD is not later than the time remaining until the earliest expiration date of any API or 6 months, whichever is earlier.
Water-Containing Oral Formulations	The BUD is not later than 14 days when stored at controlled cold temperatures.
Water-Containing Topical/Dermal and Mucosal Liquid and Semisolid Formulations	The BUD is not later than 30 days.

Handling Hazardous Drugs

USP 800 was published in February 2016 to provide guidance on ways to protect staff from hazardous drug exposure. The standards do not need to be implemented at this time, and most states have yet to finalize their state-specific requirements. Therefore, at this time, it is unlikely that this will be tested. To be safe, prior to your exam date, go to your state board website under the exam information and see if USP 800 is mentioned. RxPrep will release updates on USP 800 when we know it is required.

DISPENSING UNDER SPECIAL CIRCUMSTANCES

Conscience or Moral Clauses

The pharmacist's right to refuse dispensing certain medications (e.g., emergency contraception, oral contraceptives, abortion pills, erectile dysfunction drugs, medications used for physician-assisted suicide) based on the pharmacist's religious or moral beliefs has been a controversial issue. Some states have issued refusal or conscience clauses allowing pharmacists to refuse dispensing prescriptions based on personal values.

---

41   The BUD dates are provided in USP Chapter 795, Revision Bulletin of January 2014, available at www.usp.org

In some states (Colorado, Florida, Illinois, Maine and Tennessee) there are broad refusal clauses in state legislation that apply to all healthcare providers in general. In some states, including California, a pharmacist must dispense a prescription despite moral objection, unless the employer approves the refusal and an alternate pharmacist can provide the medication in a timely manner. In other states, such as New Jersey, refusal is prohibited on moral, religious or ethical grounds, in all circumstances. The National Conference of State Legislators (NCSL) wrote a summary in 2012 of the moral conscious clauses in the different states, which can be found at the link below.[42]

If your state has enacted legislation concerning pharmacist conscience clauses list the treatments involved and alternate methods, if stipulated, to provide the patients with the medication:

Requirements for Death with Dignity

Currently, the states of Oregon, Washington, Vermont, and California have Death with Dignity laws, which allow mentally competent, terminally ill adult state residents to voluntarily request for physician-assisted death and receive a prescription medication to end their life in a quick and painless manner.[43]

Terminally ill patients who wish to obtain a prescription under Oregon, Washington, Vermont or California law must be a resident of one of the four states and follow a series of steps in order to be permitted to take this course of action:

Death with Dignity requirements:

- 18 years of age or older

- A resident of a state permitting physician-assisted death

- Capable of making and communicating healthcare decisions for him/herself

- Diagnosed with a terminal illness that will lead to death within 6 months

- Two physicians must determine whether the above criteria have been met

---

42 *Moral conscious clause information can be found on the state board websites. A summary is provided at http://www.ncsl.org/research/health/pharmacist-conscience-clauses-laws-and-information.aspx (accessed 2015 Aug 5).*
43 *http://www.deathwithdignity.org/access-acts (accessed 2015 Jul 30).*

Timeline it takes for a patient to receive medication:

■ Patient makes first oral request to the physician

■ After at least 15 days from the initial request, the patient makes a second oral request to the physician

■ Patient makes a written request to the physician

■ After at least 48 hours from the written request, the patient may pick up the prescribed medications from the pharmacy

Medication Provisions During Declaration of Disaster or Emergency

The Emergency Prescription Assistance Program (EPAP) is a federal program managed by the Department of Health and Human Services, which provides a way for pharmacies to process claims for prescription medications and limited durable medical equipment (DME) provided to uninsured individuals from a disaster area declared by the U.S. President.[44] Claims for individuals with private insurance (e.g., individual health insurance coverage or employer-sponsored coverage), public insurance (e.g., Medicare, Medicaid), or other third party coverage, are not eligible for payment under the EPAP. Claims will be processed for a specific period of time to be determined under the EPAP activation.

Eligible individuals may be provided essential pharmaceutical and DME written prescription assistance limited to a one time, 30-day supply for a medication to treat an acute condition, to replace maintenance prescription drugs or medical equipment lost as a direct result of a disaster event or as a secondary result of loss or damage caused while in transit from the emergency site to the designated shelter facility, at no cost to the patient. Enrolled pharmacies must check for other forms of health insurance coverage at the point of sale to determine eligibility.

In order to receive prescription medications and/or DME, eligible individuals must have one of the following:

■ New prescription from a licensed healthcare practitioner

■ Current prescription bottle

■ Prescription called in by a licensed healthcare practitioner

■ Proof of an existing prescription

44   http://www.phe.gov/Preparedness/planning/epap/Pages/pharmacies.aspx (accessed 2015 Jul 30).

Enrolled pharmacies must dispense the generic form of medication unless otherwise indicated as Brand Medically Necessary (BMN) or Dispense as Written (DAW) by the licensed healthcare provider.

Telepharmacy

States that have patients in remote, rural areas have enacted regulations for telemedicine and telepharmacy to help improve healthcare delivery to underserved communities. These regulations allow the practice of virtual pharmacy using remote order verification, automated dispensing systems (ADS), videoconferencing, telephones, and the Internet. Telepharmacy provides pharmacists with a means to verify prescriptions, perform drug utilization reviews, and counsel patients remotely. State laws usually require remote telepharmacy sites to have a pharmacy license in order to receive third party reimbursement.

Patients bring prescriptions to the remote sites, which are staffed by pharmacy technicians or nurses. The central pharmacist supervises the workflow over a teleconferencing system (in real-time) and verifies prescriptions transmitted from the rural site. The prescription label and prepackaged medication are then dispensed from the ADS at the remote site. The pharmacy technician scans the barcode, attaches the label, and dispenses the medication to the patient. Finally, the pharmacist at the central location counsels the patient through a real-time video.

VACCINE ADMINISTRATION

Pharmacists play an important role in disease prevention by advocating and administering immunizations.[45] The pharmacist's authority to administer vaccines is determined by each state's laws and regulations governing pharmacy practice. All 50 states permit some type of vaccine administration by pharmacists as part of their scope of pharmacy practice.

---

45   Refer to the American Society of Hospital Pharmacists "best practices" available at https://www.ashp.org/DocLibrary/ BestPractices/SpecificGdlImmun.aspx (accessed 2015 Jul 23).

Vaccine administration may occur pursuant to individual prescription orders or through standing orders or protocols. The Centers for Disease Control (CDC) Advisory Committee on Immunization Practices (ACIP) encourages pharmacists and other healthcare providers to establish standing order programs in long-term care facilities, home healthcare agencies, hospitals, clinics, workplaces, and managed care organizations. The Centers for Medicare and Medicaid Services (CMS) no longer requires a physician order for influenza or pneumococcal immunizations administered in participating hospitals, long-term care facilities, or home healthcare agencies.[46] State-specific protocols or standing-order programs can be developed with state pharmacy associations, boards of pharmacy, and health departments.

In order to provide immunizations, a pharmacist must have taken a comprehensive training program which includes:

■ The epidemiology of and patient populations at risk for vaccine-preventable diseases

■ Public health goals for immunization (e.g., local, regional, state, and federal goals)

■ Vaccine safety (e.g., risk–benefit analysis)

■ Screening for contraindications and precautions of vaccination

■ Vaccine stability, transportation and storage requirements

■ Immunologic drug interactions

■ Vaccine dosing, including interpreting recommended immunization schedules and patient immunization records, and determining proper dosing intervals and the feasibility of simultaneous administration of multiple vaccines

■ Proper dose preparation and injection techniques

■ Signs and symptoms of adverse reactions to vaccines, adverse reaction reporting, and emergency procedures, such as basic and advanced cardiac life support (BCLS and ACLS)

■ Documentation

■ Reporting to the primary care provider or local health department and the vaccine registry

■ Billing

---

46 https://www.cms.gov/Medicare/Prevention/Immunizations/Providerresources.html (accessed 2015 Jul 28).

RETURN, DISPOSAL, OR REUSE OF MEDICATIONS

Returning or Disposing Prescription Medication to the Supplier

The FDA permits pharmacies to return prescription drugs to wholesalers and manufacturers as long as there is proper recordkeeping. Prescription drugs that are outdated, damaged, deteriorated, misbranded, or adulterated must be physically separated from other prescription drugs until they are destroyed or returned to the supplier.[47]

Opened prescription drug containers must be identified as opened (this is often done in the pharmacy by marking an "X" on the container), and kept physically separated from the unopened containers if they are sent to be destroyed or are returned to the supplier.

If the storage conditions under which a prescription drug has been returned cast any doubt on the drug's safety, identity, strength, quality, or purity, then the drug should be returned to the wholesaler or manufacturer, or sent to disposal, unless the contents can be tested and the quality has been confirmed.

Returns from the Pharmacy Will Call (Pick Up) Area

If a patient has not picked up filled medication (which has not left the pharmacy premise), the unclaimed medication can be returned to stock, provided that there is an expiration date on the label. The returned medication can be combined with a stock bottle only if they have the same lot number.

Many states or companies have implemented their own policies on unclaimed medications, such as requiring courtesy calls if medication is unclaimed and a time duration before the medication can be returned to stock.

My state requires a courtesy call if a patient has not picked up their medication within a given time frame.   Yes / No

If yes, specify the time frame: _____

My state does not permit medications to be returned to the shelf until this amount of time has passed: _____

14 days NY

---

47   http://www.accessdata.fda.gov/scripts/cdrh/cfdocs/cfcfr/CFRSearch.cfm?fr=205.50 (accessed 2015 Jul 28).

Charitable Programs

Commonly, states permit prescription drugs in single use or sealed packaging from state programs, nursing homes and medical facilities to be provided to low-income residents who cannot afford their drugs. This helps offset the costs of providing healthcare to uninsured patients in emergency rooms and clinics. The laws include some restrictions to secure the drug integrity, including:[48]

- Drugs must be in the original, unopened, sealed, and tamper-evident unit-dose packaging

- Drugs must not be expired

- The expiration date must be visible and at least 6 months from the donation date (in most states)

- Controlled substances cannot be donated—these are excluded (in most states)

- A state-licensed pharmacist or pharmacy is part of the verification and distribution process

- The patient receiving the donated drugs requires a valid prescription

Drug Donations to Cancer or Other Repository Programs

A handful of states (Colorado, Florida, Kentucky, Minnesota, and Nebraska) have enacted programs specifically for accepting and distributing unused cancer-related prescription drugs.

Patients Returning Previously Dispensed Medications to the Pharmacy

On occasion, patients come back to the pharmacy asking to return prescription medications. This can be due to a variety of reasons: the dose may have changed, the course of treatment has been completed, or the patient simply has too much of the drug. The FDA compliance policy guide recommends that a pharmacist should not accept returned drugs from patients and return it to the pharmacy shelves (or pharmacy stock) after it has left the pharmacy premises.[49] This is because the pharmacist would no longer have any assurance of the strength, quality, purity or identity of the drugs. Many state boards of pharmacy have regulations prohibiting this practice. The pharmacist dispensing a drug is legally responsible for the adulteration that may be present if the returned drugs are combined with the pharmacy stock and subsequently re-dispensed to other patients.

48   http://www.ncsl.org/research/health/state-prescription-drug-return-reuse-and-recycling.aspx (accessed 2015 Jul 29).
49   http://www.fda.gov/ICECI/ComplianceManuals/CompliancePolicyGuidanceManual/ucm074399.htm (accessed 2015 Jul 29).

Disposal of Prescription Medication by the Ultimate User

Community-based drug "take-back" programs are good options for patients to dispose of prescription medications. The take-back program offered by the DEA was temporarily discontinued but has now been restarted.[50] Patients should check on the DEA's website or contact their city or county government's household trash and recycling service to see if a local take-back program is available.

There are also new rules that allow authorized facilities, such as pharmacies, to collect unused and unwanted prescription drugs, including controlled substances. Previously, controlled substances could only be returned to a location with law enforcement present. A facility that is willing to collect unused drugs will need to apply for a permit.

Patients should follow any specific disposal instructions on the prescription drug labeling or patient information that accompanies the drug. Drugs should not be flushed down the sink or toilet unless instructed by the prescription labeling.

If no disposal instructions are given on the prescription drug labeling and no local take-back program is available, patients should dispose of drugs in the household trash following these steps:

- Remove the drugs from their original containers and mix them with an undesirable substance, such as kitty litter or used coffee grounds (this makes the drug less appealing to children and pets, and unrecognizable to people who may intentionally go through the trash seeking drugs)

- Place the mixture in a sealable bag, empty can, or other container, then discard in the trash

Some drugs are especially harmful if taken by someone other than the person for whom the medication was prescribed, and some of the medications that have the highest risk will include specific disposal instructions on the labeling. This may include instructions to immediately flush unused medication or used medication patches down the toilet. For example, too much fentanyl can cause severe respiratory depression and lead to death. Leftover and used fentanyl patches should be flushed down the toilet.

It is not acceptable practice to flush drugs down the toilet except where the risk is high. Drugs that can be flushed are included in the Disposal of Prescription Drugs chapter of the RxPrep Course Book. See the dispensing controlled substances section of this booklet for more information on disposal of controlled substances.

50   http://www.deadiversion.usdoj.gov/drug_disposal/takeback/ *(accessed 2015 Jul 29).*

MANUFACTURER DRUG SAMPLES GIVEN TO PRESCRIBERS TO PROVIDE TO PATIENTS

The practice of drug company sales representatives providing drug samples to prescribers in order to push sales for their drugs has caused significant issues for safe drug delivery for many years. They also help steer use toward expensive brand drugs when less expensive generic alternatives may be available. The drug samples that are given to prescribers can become expired, adulterated, misbranded, or diverted, since they may not have been kept in proper storage requirements and may have been repackaged or relabeled.

The Prescription Drug Marketing Act (PDMA) regulated manufacturer activities to prevent drug diversion, and included restrictions on distributing drug samples. Samples can only be given to prescribers or to a hospital pharmacy or other healthcare entity at the written request of the prescriber. A "healthcare entity" is defined to specifically exclude retail pharmacies.

Sample drugs must be stored separately from other drug inventory. Many states require the prescriber's office to maintain receipts of samples received. Drug samples are different from "starter packs," and from drugs that are provided free of charge, or at a reduced price, pursuant to an indigent patient program.

RESALE OF DISCOUNTED PRESCRIPTION DRUGS

Many hospitals and health maintenance organizations are able to purchase drugs at a discounted rate due to competitive bidding and nonprofit status. In the past, additional drug was ordered or excess drug inventory was found to be present, and was resold. The institution made money by selling the drugs to community pharmacies or other healthcare facilities at a profit.

The resale of prescription drugs was prohibited by PDMA, with these exceptions:

- Sales or purchases to other facilities within the same organization

- Sales to nonprofit affiliates

- For emergency reasons

PRESCRIPTION MEDICATION LOSS OR THEFT

In the event of a robbery, the pharmacy staff should not resist, either verbally or physically. The staff should never try to apprehend or restrain the robber. Robbers are often armed. The staff members should take notice of the appearance of the robber in order to provide a description to law enforcement later. The pharmacy staff should sound the alarm and call the police when it is safe to do so. Doors should be locked immediately to prevent re-entry.

Theft or loss of controlled substances must be documented on a DEA Form 106. See the dispensing controlled substances section of this booklet for more information on reporting loss or theft of controlled substances. The DEA recommends the following measures to be aware of and reduce the risk of theft:[51]

■ Maintain an inventory of controlled substances

■ Monitor staff for changes in behavior or mood

■ Contact law enforcement if theft is suspected

■ Perform criminal background checks for all pharmacy staff

■ Give alarm codes for all personnel

■ Limit issuance of pharmacy keys

■ Change locks, alarm codes, and safe combinations periodically

■ Ensure lighting is adequate in the pharmacy area at all times

■ Place opioids out of sight

■ Have obvious surveillance or cameras in plain sight

■ Install duress alarms

■ Have adequate, physical barriers to prevent unsolicited entrance behind the pharmacy counter

■ Install steel window curtains and doors

RECORDKEEPING OF PRESCRIPTION MEDICATION

Most states mandate that prescription records must be maintained for at least two years. Some states may have stricter requirements; the longest is Arizona, which requires prescription records be kept for 7 years.

My state requires prescriptions records to be kept for this number of years: _____

---

51   http://www.deadiversion.usdoj.gov/mtgs/pharm_awareness/conf_2013/march_2013/browning.pdf *(accessed 2015 Jul 30).*

MAINTAINING PEDIGREES TO ENSURE THE QUALITY OF DRUGS

There is an increasing prevalence of counterfeit, misbranded, adulterated, and diverted prescription drugs showing up in the United States. To prevent these drugs from entering the legitimate drug supply, the Drug Supply Chain Security Act was passed in 2013, which outlines critical steps to build an electronic, interoperable "track and trace" system by November 2023 to identify and trace certain prescription drugs as they are distributed within the United States.[52]

Manufacturers, wholesale distributors, pharmacies and repackagers (collectively referred to as "trading partners") are required to provide the subsequent purchaser with product tracing information when engaging in transactions involving certain prescription drugs. This means that anytime the drug is moved from one place to another, paperwork must follow.[53]

Pharmacies must be able to capture and maintain transaction information (TI), transaction history (TH), and a transaction statement (TS), in paper or electronic form, for each drug product received for six years from the date of the transaction.

---

52 http://www.fda.gov/downloads/Drugs/GuidanceComplianceRegulatoryInformation/Guidances/UCM453225.pdf (accessed 2016 July 6).
53 http://www.fda.gov/Drugs/DrugSafety/DrugIntegrityandSupplyChainSecurity/DrugSupplyChainSecurityAct/ (accessed 2016 July 6).

5

Controlled Substances

LAWS, RULES, AND REGULATIONS

Controlled Substances Act

This section begins with a chart of the most common DEA forms and their purpose.

DEA FORM #	PURPOSE
224	Registration Form for Retail Pharmacies, Hospitals/Clinics, Practitioners, Teaching Institutions, or Mid-Level Practitioners
225	Registration Form for Manufacturers, Distributors, Researchers, Analytical Laboratories, Importers, Exporters
363	Registration Form for Narcotic Treatment Programs
222	Ordering Schedule I and II Drugs
106	Reporting the Theft or Significant Loss of Controlled Substances
41	Record of Controlled Substances Destroyed

The U.S. Attorney General, under authority provided by the CSA, is responsible for the enforcement of federal law requirements for the manufacture, importation, possession, use and distribution of controlled substances, which are divided into 5 schedules as shown in the following table. States can classify substances in stricter categories. The DEA works with the FDA to make decisions about the schedule in which a controlled substance is placed. Sometimes, a drug is moved to a different schedule (such as the recent move of all hydrocodone-containing products into schedule II) if the perceived risks involving the drug have changed. This process is known as reclassification. The DEA is primarily concerned with diversion, whereas the FDA is primarily concerned with legitimate medical need and safety (primarily due to overdose).

This section reviews the Controlled Substance Act (CSA), which sets the regulations for controlled substances.[54] Pharmacists can use the DEA's Pharmacists Manual as a guide to interpret the CSA and how it applies to pharmacy practice. State laws may not be more lenient than federal requirements, but they can be stricter. For example, tramadol is federally classified as a schedule IV drug.

If tramadol abuse is common in a particular state, the state board of pharmacy may opt to classify tramadol as schedule III. They would not be permitted to move the drug into schedule V.

54   The PDF of the DEA Pharmacists Manual can be downloaded at www.deadiversion.usdoj.gov (accessed 2015 Aug 6).

Classification of Controlled Substances

The higher the potential for abuse, the lower the schedule number. Schedule I drugs have the highest potential for abuse and are considered to have no accepted medical use. Drugs in this category (such as heroin and LSD) may be used for research purposes, but are most commonly used illicitly (illegally/unlawfully). Marijuana is an exception; it is classified as schedule I according to the DEA, but is available in an increasing number of states. Marijuana is not dispensed in pharmacies and remains illegal under federal law. Most schedule II-V drugs are dispensed in pharmacies with a prescription. Select schedule V drugs (primarily cough syrups) can be sold without a prescription in some states as long as certain requirements are met, such as keeping a logbook of sales.

Codeine is unusual because the different formulations are in different schedules: schedule II if it is a single agent, schedule III if it is formulated as part of a combination product, and schedule V if it is formulated as a combination cough syrup. In contrast, hydrocodone is schedule II in all single and combination products and tramadol is schedule IV in all single and combination products as well.

Generally, most controlled substances of the same pharmacological class will be in the same schedule. However, barbiturates can be schedule II, III, or IV. Single agent formulations of amobarbital, pentobarbital, and secobarbital are schedule II. If amobarbital, secobarbital, or pentobarbital are formulated as a suppository or as a combination product with a non-controlled substance, then it is schedule III. Butabarbital is schedule III. Butabarbital is not to be confused with butalbital. Butalbital is currently only available in combination with non-controlled substances, and is schedule III. Phenobarbital is schedule IV. Phenobarbital is not to be confused with pentobarbital.

It will not be possible to answer some of the questions on the MPJE without knowledge of the categories for the controlled substances. The classification of the drug will determine the requirements for ordering, labeling, refills, emergency fills, and inventory and recordkeeping.

If your state classifies select drugs in a different schedule than the federal classification, list the drugs and the schedules:

Controlled Substance Schedules

SCHEDULE	EXAMPLES
C-I	Heroin
	Gamma-hydroxybutyric acid or GHB (the sodium salt form, sodium oxybate, is C-III)
	Lysergic acid diethylamide or LSD
	Marijuana or cannabis
	Peyote
	Mescaline
	3,4-methylenedioxy-methamphetamine or MDMA ("Ecstasy")
C-II	Cocaine
	Sufentanil (*Sufenta*)
	Fentanyl (*Duragesic, Actiq, Fentora, Onsolis, Subsys, Lazanda, Abstral*) Alfenta
	Methadone (*Dolophine, Methadose*)
	Levo-alpha acetyl methadol or LAAM
	Hydromorphone (*Dilaudid*)
	Morphine (*MS Contin*)
	Oxycodone containing products (*Percocet, Percodan, OxyContin*)
	Hydrocodone containing products (*Zohydro ER, Hysingla ER, Norco, Vicodin, TussiCaps, Tussionex*)
	Codeine
	Tapentadol (*Nucynta*)
	Meperidine (*Demerol*)
	Methylphenidate (*Ritalin, Concerta*)
	Amphetamine containing products (*Dexedrine, Adderall*)
	Lisdexamfetamine (*Vyvanse*)
	Pentobarbital (*Nembutal*)
	Secobarbital (*Seconal*)
	Amobarbital (*Amytal Sodium*)
C-III	Codeine/acetaminophen (*Tylenol with Codeine #3, Tylenol with Codeine #4*)
	Dronabinol (*Marinol*)
	Anabolic steroids such as testosterone (*AndroGel*) (C-II NY) + chorionic gonadotropin
	Buprenorphine (*Suboxone, Subutex*)
	Butabarbital (*Butisol*)
	Butalbital/Acetaminophen/Caffeine/Codeine (*Fioricet with Codeine*)
	Butalbital/Aspirin/Caffeine/Codeine (*Fiorinal with Codeine*)
	Butalbital/Aspirin/Caffeine (*Fiorinal*)
	Sodium oxybate (*Xyrem*)
	Ketamine (*Ketalar*)
	Benzphetamine (*Regimex*)
	Phendimetrazine (*Bontril PDM*) = Anorectic, promotes wgt loss
	Perampanel (*Fycompa*) = antiepileptic

SCHEDULE	EXAMPLES
C-IV	Zolpidem (*Ambien*)
	Zaleplon (*Sonata*)
	Eszopiclone (*Lunesta*)
	Benzodiazepines such as lorazepam (*Ativan*), diazepam (*Valium*), alprazolam (*Xanax*) *NYS (treat as C-II)*
	Modafinil (*Provigil*)
	Armodafinil (*Nuvigil*)
	Carisoprodol (*Soma*)
	Tramadol containing products (*Ultram, Ultracet, ConZip*)
	Phentermine/topiramate (*Qsymia*)
	Butorphanol (*Stadol*)
	Suvorexant (*Belsomra*)
	Diethylpropion (*Tenuate*)
	Phentermine (*Adipex-P, Suprenza*)
	Lorcaserin (*Belviq*)
	Difenoxin/atropine (*Mofeten*)
	Phenobarbital
	Propoxyphene (*Darvocet, Darvon*), fenfluramine (*Pondimin*) - both discontinued
C-V	Codeine containing cough syrups (codeine/promethazine, codeine/promethazine/phenylephrine, codeine/guaifenisen, others)
	Pregabalin (*Lyrica*)
	Ezogabine (*Potiga*)
	Lacosamide (*Vimpat*)
	Diphenoxylate/atropine (*Lomotil*)
	Difenoxin/atropine (*Mofeten half strength*) – discontinued

Maximum Limits and Set Opioid Amounts

The scheduling of some drugs depend on the opioid concentration. There are some drugs available in a few of the categories that the DEA defines in the following table, including *Paregoric* (an oral liquid containing morphine 2 mg/5 mL) and *Tylenol with Codeine* (which contains acetaminophen and 15-60 mg of codeine per tablet). However, in some of the categories, the drugs have been discontinued or are rarely used.

SCHEDULE	NOT MORE THAN (NMT) QUANTITY LIMIT
Schedule III	Not more than 1.8 g of codeine per 100 mL or not more than 90 mg per dosage unit when combined with an equal or greater quantity of an isoquinoline alkaloid of opium
Typically, these are calculated based on the Rule of Three as many of these numbers are divisible by 3.	Not more than 1.8 g of codeine per 100 mL or not more than 90 mg per dosage unit when combined with one or more active non-narcotic ingredient
	Not more than 1.8 g of dihydrocodeine per 100 mL or not more than 90 mg per dosage unit when combined with one or more active non-narcotic ingredient
	Not more than 300 mg of ethylmorphine per 100 mL or not more than 15 mg per dosage unit when combined with one or more active non-narcotic ingredient
	Not more than 500 mg of opium per 100 mL or per 100 g or not more than 25 mg per dosage unit when combined with one or more active non-narcotic ingredient
	Not more than 50 mg of morphine per 100 mL or per 100 g when combined with one or more active non-narcotic ingredient
Schedule IV	Not more than 1 mg difenoxin and not less than 25 mcg of atropine sulfate per dosage unit
Schedule V	Not more than 200 mg of codeine per 100 mL or per 100 g when combined with one or more active non-narcotic ingredient (such as *Robitussin AC*, promethazine/codeine cough syrup)
Typically, these are calculated based on the Rule of Five as many of these numbers are divisible by 5.	Not more than 100 mg of dihydrocodeine per 100 mL or per 100 g when combined with one or more active non-narcotic ingredient (such as dihydrocodeine/chlorpheniramine/phenylprine cough syrup)
	Not more than 100 mg of ethylmorphine per 100 mL or per 100 g when combined with one or more active non-narcotic ingredient
	Not more than 2.5 mg of diphenoxylate and not less than 25 mcg of atropine sulfate per dosage unit (e.g., *Lomotil*)
	Not more than 100 mg of opium per 100 mL or per 100 g when combined with one or more active non-narcotic ingredient
	Not more than 0.5 mg of difenoxin and not less than 25 mcg of atropine sulfate per dosage unit

ORDERING CONTROLLED SUBSTANCES

DEA Form 222

Form 222 (or its electronic equivalent) is required for each distribution, purchase, or transfer of schedule I or II drugs. A pharmacist would usually use the Form 222 to order schedule II drugs, sell or lend schedule II drugs to another pharmacy or prescriber, borrow schedule II drugs from another pharmacy, or return controlled substances to the wholesaler or reverse distributer.

The Form 222 is a serially numbered (with a consecutive number series), triplicate form, and is pre-printed with the pharmacy's name, address, DEA number, and the schedules of controlled substances that can be ordered by the registrant. The colors of the triplicate forms are brown (Copy 1), green (Copy 2), and blue (Copy 3). If a registration terminates or the pre-printed name and address needs to be revised, the unused forms are returned to the DEA and new forms will be required.

The registrant requesting/receiving the schedule II drugs (e.g., the pharmacy) will keep Copy 3 and send Copies 1 and 2 to the supplier. Upon delivery of the controlled substances to the recipient (e.g., the pharmacy), the registrant supplying the drugs (e.g., the drug wholesaler) will forward Copy 2 to the DEA. Note that the pharmacy keeps Copy 3 when purchasing the controlled substances from the wholesaler - but the pharmacy will keep Copy 1 when returning drugs to a wholesaler or sending drugs to a reverse distributor for disposal since, in these cases, the pharmacy is "supplying" the drugs. The table below outlines who must keep which copy of the Form 222 in different scenarios.

ACTION	COPY 1 (BROWN)	COPY 2 (GREEN)	COPY 3 (BLUE)
The pharmacy orders schedule II drugs from a wholesaler	Supplier	DEA	Pharmacy
The pharmacy returns unused schedule II drugs back to a supplier	Pharmacy	DEA	Supplier
The pharmacy sends unused schedule II drugs back to reverse distributor for disposal	Pharmacy	DEA	Reverse distributor
The pharmacy sells or lends schedule II drugs to another pharmacy that is out of stock and needs the drugs to dispense a prescription	Supplying pharmacy	DEA	Receiving Pharmacy
The pharmacy sells or lends schedule II drugs to a physician for administration or dispensing to a patient	Pharmacy	DEA	Physician

A Form 222 is not required if drug products are transferred from a central fill pharmacy to its retail pharmacy or when the schedule II drug is being dispensed to the patient. Other than these two exceptions, Form 222 is to document every distribution, purchase, or transfer of schedule II drugs.

Requesting DEA Form 222

Initial Forms 222 can be requested on the Form 224 , which is the application for initial DEA registration. Once a registrant has received a DEA registration number, additional Forms 222 can be ordered on the DEA website or by calling the DEA Headquarters Registration Unit or the nearest DEA Field Office.

Ordering Schedule II Drugs with DEA Form 222

Schedule I drugs may be used for research with permission from the DEA and FDA but are neither ordered by pharmacies nor prescribed by healthcare providers. This section on how to use the Form 222 focuses on schedule II drugs. The Form 222 or the electronic equivalent (the Controlled Substance Ordering System or CSOS) is required for the distribution, purchase, or transfer of schedule II drugs. The electronic CSOS can be used for ordering all schedules (I-V).

1. The Form 222 must be completed with a typewriter, ink pen, or indelible (non-erasable) pencil. If the form is filled out by hand with an ink pen or indelible pencil, the purchaser must press firmly to ensure that all three forms will be legible.

2. Each item must be written on a separate line with a total of 10 lines on each form. A maximum of 10 items can be ordered. Lines cannot be skipped. The purchaser must fill out the name and address of the supplier, only one supplier can be used on a form. There are three columns for each drug that must be complete:

    ■ The number of packages (e.g., 25)

    ■ The size of the package (e.g., 946 mL)

    ■ The name (brand or generic) and dosage (e.g., methadone HCl 10 mg/mL)

3. The purchaser can leave the NDC entry blank since the supplier may not have the exact product the pharmacy requested, and can substitute a different package size or select a different manufacturer. The same drug in a different size package or from a different manufacturer will have a different NDC number. These substitutions are permitted as long as the quantity provided does not exceed the amount ordered. For example, *Norco* 7.5/325 mg is supplied as bottles of 100 and 500 tablets. If the pharmacy orders 5 of the 500-count bottles and the distributor does not have the 500 count, they can provide 25 of the 100-count bottles. Either option will provide the purchaser with 2500 tablets, which is the quantity that was ordered. Each of the different size bottles and each different manufacturer will have a different NDC number, which is why it is more convenient to leave it blank so the supplier can fill in the NDC number for the exact item that is sent to the purchaser.

4. The last line completed must be indicated in the space provided on the form, which will be the total number of different items ordered. This field must be completed and will be 10 or less, since there are 10 lines on the form. If this is left blank or does not match the number of lines that have been completed, it will be returned to the pharmacy. In the sample Form 222 that follows, since three items are ordered, the purchaser must record "3" in the space marked "last line completed".

5. The Form 222 must be signed and dated by the person authorized to sign the registration application or a person who has been granted power of attorney. If the form is not signed and dated, it will be returned to the pharmacy. tration application or a person who has been granted power of attorney. If the form is not signed and dated, it will be returned to the pharmacy.

6.   If a mistake is made, the purchaser must write "Void" on the Form 222 and begin again with a new Form 222.

7.   The Form 222 must be filled completely and legibly or it cannot be filled and will be returned to the purchaser. The Form 222 will be sent back if alterations or cross-outs are present, if the drug name, strength, size, quantify is missing or if the date or signature is missing. Minor errors (for example, misspelling "methodone" for methadone) could be reasonably corrected by the distributor. However, it is best to avoid even simple errors.

8.   Once completed, the purchaser keeps Copy 3 (blue Copy) sends Copy 1 and 2 (brown and green Copy) to the supplier. The first two Copies must remain together, with the carbon intact. If the top two Copies are not attached, the supplier cannot accept the order and will return the Copies to the pharmacy.

9.   On Copies 1 and 2, the supplier records the number of containers furnished per item along with date of shipment. If the supplier cannot provide the entire quantity, the supplier can provide a partial shipment and supply the balance within 60 days from the date the Form 222 was completed by the purchaser. The supplier maintains Copy 1 for its files and sends Copy 2 to the DEA by the end of the month during which the order was fulfilled. If the supplier cannot fulfill the order within the specified time limit, the supplier can endorse the order to another supplier to fill.

10. Shipments of controlled substances can be sent only to the current DEA registered address.

11. The supplier delivers the scheduled drugs to the purchaser in its own container, which is separate from the non-scheduled and OTC drugs. The order is checked in by the pharmacist who will record the number of packages received and the date received on Copy 3.

12. Federal law requires the purchaser to keep copy 3 of the Form 222 (and all scheduled drug forms) for at least 2 years. A state can require purchasers to keep records for a longer period of time. All records related to schedule II drugs (orders, invoices, prescriptions, inventory records) are kept separate from other forms.

Cancelling or Voiding DEA Form 222

If the supplier cannot fulfill the order or if the order form is illegible, incomplete, or altered, then the supplier returns Copies 1 and 2 to the purchaser with a rationale for not filling the order. The purchaser must keep all three copies.

A supplier can void part or all of an order by notifying the purchaser in writing. The supplier must draw a line through the cancelled items on Copies 1 and 2 of the Form 222 and print "Void" in the space provided for the number of items shipped.

A purchaser can cancel all or part of an order by notifying the supplier in writing. The supplier indicates the cancellation on Copies 1 and 2 by drawing a line through the cancelled item/s and writing "Cancelled" in the space where they would usually put the number of items shipped.

Lost or Stolen DEA Form 222

If the Form 222 that was sent to the supplier becomes lost or stolen, the purchaser must re-order with a new form. The pharmacist must prepare a statement that the order was not received, and include the serial number of the lost or stolen form, and the date of the loss. This statement must be attached to the new order form and sent to the supplier. Copy 3 of the new and the original Form 222 and the statement are filed together. If the supplier subsequently receives the original order form, it is marked as "not accepted" and returned to the purchaser who files the original Copies 1 and 2 with the original Copy 3.

SAMPLE DEA FORM-222
SHADED SECTIONS ARE FILLED IN BY THE NTP
WHEN PLACING AN ORDER

See Reverse of PURCHASER'S Copy of Instructions	No order form may be issued for Schedule I and II substances unless a completed application form has been received, (21 CFR 1305.04).	OMB APPROVAL No. 1117-0010

TO: *(Name of Supplier)* **Methadone Supplier** STREET ADDRESS **21 Xyz Lane**

CITY and STATE **Anytown, FL 22312**	DATE **MM/DD/YYYY**	TO BE FILLED IN BY SUPPLIER SUPPLIERS DEA REGISTRATION No.

TO BE FILLED IN BY PURCHASER

L I N E No.	No. of Packages	Size of Package	Name of Item	National Drug Code	Packages Shipped	Date Shipped
1	25	946 ml	Methadone HCl 10mg/ml			
2	5	100	Methadone HCl Tablets 10mg			
3	20	4 x 25	Methadone HCl diskettes 40mg			
4						
5						
6						
7						
8						
9						
10						

3 ◄ LAST LINE COMPLETED *(MUST BE 10 OR LESS)*	SIGNATURE OR PURCHASER OR ATTORNEY OR AGENT	*John Doe*

Date Issued **MM/DD/YYYY**	DEA Registration No. **RW0000000**	Name and Address of Registrant **Who Treatment Center** **123 Whatever Lane** **Whereami, FL 12345**
Schedules **2**		
Registered as a **NTP BOTH**	No. of this Order Form **1234567890**	***** TO BE USED FOR METHADONE AND LAAM ONLY *****

DEA Form-222 (Oct. 1992)

U.S. OFFICIAL ORDER FORMS - SCHEDULES I & II
DRUG ENFORCEMENT ADMINISTRATION
SUPPLIER'S Copy 1

Sample DEA Form 222 completed by the purchaser

Electronic Controlled Substance Ordering System

The electronic Controlled Substance Ordering System (CSOS) is the electronic equivalent to Form 222. CSOS is used to order schedule I and II drugs and, unlike Form 222, can be used to order controlled drugs in schedules III, IV and V and non-controlled drugs.[55] Each Form 222 can only be used to order up to 10 items; the CSOS has no limits on the quantity of items to be ordered. Utilizing CSOS reduces ordering errors, requires less paperwork and reduces administrative costs. Drug delivery is faster with CSOS than with the paper form, which requires additional time for the supplier to receive the form from the pharmacy. With CSOS, the purchaser can order the drugs, have the order electronically sent to the supplier within the same business day, and the supplier can deliver the order to the purchaser by the next business day. Ordering through CSOS improves inventory control. There is less stockpiling and less waiting time to fill up a paper order form. Orders can be placed more often for fewer items.

	PAPER DEA FORM 222	ELECTRONIC CSOS
Limit of items per order	10 items	No limits
What drugs can be ordered	Schedules I, II	Schedules I, II, III, IV, V, and non-scheduled
Typical turnaround time	1-7 business days	1-2 business days
Type of signature used	Wet (handwritten) signature	Digital signature
Can the order be endorsed to another supplier?	Yes	No
When must supplier report transaction to DEA?	By the end of the month during which the order was filled	Within 2 business days of filling the order

CSOS utilizes Public Key Infrastructure (PKI) technology to securely exchange data. The purchaser (such as the pharmacy) enrolls with the DEA to receive a CSOS digital certificate and public-private key pairs. The public key is used to encrypt data, and the private key is used to decrypt data, which enables the purchaser and supplier to securely exchange data.

A CSOS digital certificate is essentially an authorized digital identity that contains information about the registrant, including the name, email address, location name and address, DEA number, the schedules the registrant can order, and the expiration date of the certificate. The purchaser signs the electronic controlled substance order with the digital certificate.

---

55   http://www.deadiversion.usdoj.gov/ecomm/csos/archive/overview.pdf (accessed 2015 Jul 30).

Ordering Controlled Substances with CSOS

The registrant creates the CSOS order using DEA-approved software which is typically available through the wholesaler's online ordering website. When the order is complete, the purchaser signs it with the digital certificate and electronically transmits it to the supplier. The supplier receives the order, verifies the certificate, and fills the order. Electronic orders can not be endorsed to another supplier. The purchaser will know almost instantaneously that the supplier cannot fill all or part of an order and can simply issue a new electronic order to a different supplier. The supplier must report the order information to the DEA within 2 business days from the date the supplier received the order.

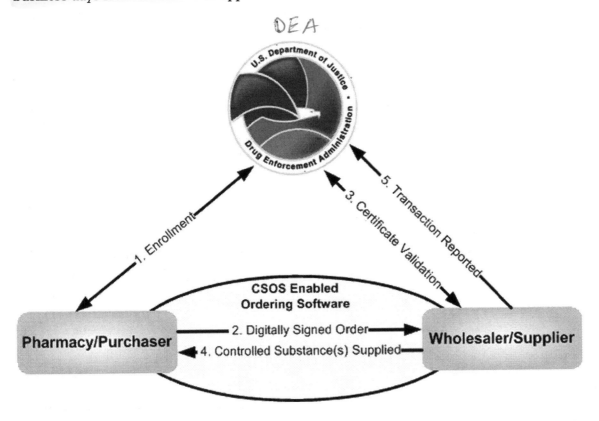

CSOS order and supply chain

Cancelling or Voiding Electronic Orders

An electronic order is invalid if any required data field is missing, if it is not signed with a DEA-sanctioned digital certificate, if the digital certificate is expired, or if the purchaser's public key will not validate the digital signature. The supplier can refuse to fill an order for any reason and must provide the purchaser with a statement of the occurrence. The purchaser must electronically link this statement to the original order. Invalid electronic orders cannot be corrected; a new order must be submitted by the purchaser.

The supplier is not required to keep a record of orders that were not filled, but the purchaser must keep an electronic copy of the voided order. If a supplier partially voids an order, the supplier must indicate in the linked record that nothing was shipped for each voided item.

Theft or Loss of Controlled Substance Orders

If an unfulfilled order from Form 222 or CSOS is lost, the purchaser must provide the supplier with the unique tracking number, the date of the loss, and a statement that the goods from the first order were never received. If the purchaser issues another order to replace the lost order, the lost order (along with the statement of loss) and the replacement order must be electronically linked.

Granting the Power of Attorney

The DEA registrant orders the controlled substances for the pharmacy with the Form 222 or CSOS. That person may not be present all the time, and can authorize others to order the controlled substances in their place by granting a power of attorney (POA). A POA is a legal document that gives the person the registrant has chosen the power to act in the registrant's place. Licensed or unlicensed individuals can be granted a POA. Multiple POAs can be issued if the registrant requires more than one substitute. The person who granted the POA may revoke it at any time. If a new registrant completes the renewal application, new power of attorney form/s will need to be completed. The POA documents are not submitted to the DEA, but must be filed with the completed Forms 222 and should be readily retrievable in the event that the pharmacy needs to provide them to an inspector. The DEA does not provide an official power of attorney form, but recommends the wording shown on the following page.

Power of Attorney

(Name of registrant) _____

(Address of registrant) _____

(DEA registration number) _____

I, _____ (name of person granting power), the undersigned, who is authorized to sign the current application for registration of the above-named registrant under the Controlled Substances Act or Controlled Substances Import and Export Act, have made, constituted, and appointed, and by these presents, do make, constitute, and appoint _____ (name of attorney-in-fact), my true and lawful attorney for me in my name, place, and stead, to execute applications for Forms 222 and to sign orders for Schedule I and II drugs, whether these orders be on Form 222 or electronic, in accordance with 21 U.S.C. 828 and Part 1305 of Title 21 of the Code of Federal Regulations. I hereby ratify and confirm all that said attorney must lawfully do or cause to be done by virtue hereof.

_____

(Signature of person granting power)

I, _____ (name of attorney-in-fact), hereby affirm that I am the person

named herein as attorney-in-fact and that the signature affixed hereto is my signature.

_____

(Signature of attorney-in-fact)

Witnesses:

1. _____   2. _____

Signed and dated on the _____ day of _____, (year), at _____.

Notice of Revocation

The foregoing power of attorney is hereby revoked by the undersigned, who is authorized to sign the current application for registration of the above-named registrant under the Controlled Substances Act or the Controlled Substances Import and Export Act. Written notice of this revocation has been given to the attorney-in-fact this same day.

_____

(Signature of person revoking power)

Witnesses:

1. _____   2. _____

Signed and dated on the _____ day of _____, (year), at _____.

Sample of a Power of Attorney Form

Ordering Schedule III-V Drugs

The registrant must keep a receipt (e.g., the invoice or packing slip) on which the registrant records the date the drugs were received and confirms that the order was accurate. These receipts must contain the name of each controlled substance, the formulation, the number of dosage units in each commercial container, and the number of containers ordered and received. These receipts must be kept in a readily retrievable manner for inspection.

PRESCRIBING AND FILLING CONTROLLED SUBSTANCES

Healthcare Providers Authorized to Prescribe Controlled Substances

A prescription for a controlled substance for a legitimate medical purpose may only be issued by a physician (MD/DO), dentist (DDS, DMD), podiatrist (DPM), veterinarian (DVM), mid-level practitioner (MLP), or other registered practitioner who is:

- Authorized to prescribe controlled substances by the jurisdiction or state in which the practitioner is licensed to practice

- Registered or exempt from DEA registration

- An agent or employee of a hospital or institution acting in the normal course of business under the registration of the hospital or institution

Only physicians have unlimited, independent prescribing authority in all states, although it is preferable to prescribe within the area of expertise. The license to practice medicine is granted by the individual states.

The prescribing authority for all other prescribers is limited to the practitioner's scope of practice in all states and may require a collaborative practice agreement with a physician. For example, naturopathic doctors (NDs) are generally limited to "natural" compounds such as vitamins, natural hormones (e.g., *Armour Thyroid*), or amino acids. The prescribing authority of mid-level practitioners (MLPs) varies by state and by type of practitioner. MLPs vary by state and can include nurse practitioners (NPs), certified nurse midwives (CNMs), anesthetist nurses (ANs), physician assistants (PAs) and optometrists (ODs).

An employee or agent (such as a nurse or office assistant), under the direct supervision of a prescriber, may communicate prescription information to a pharmacist. The agent can also prepare a prescription for the prescriber to sign and date.

My state permits the following MLPs to prescribe the following schedules of controlled substances:

MLP TYPE	SCHEDULES OF DRUGS	PRESCRIBING LIMITATIONS

Healthcare providers employed by the following organizations are exempt from DEA registration: U.S. Public Health Service, the Federal Bureau of Prisons, and the U.S. Armed Forces (Army, Air Force, Navy, Marine Corps and Coast Guard). Additionally, under the Indian Self-Determination and Education Assistance Act, institutions and employees of Indian healthcare facilities are exempt. Prescribers employed by these facilities are not be required to register with the DEA in order to write for controlled substances. Many of these practitioners will still apply for a DEA number in order to work at an outside private practice.

Prescribing Controlled Substances for Oneself or Immediate Family Members

The American Medical Association (AMA) does not recommend self-prescribing or treating immediate family members. This ethical and legal issue is discussed in detail in the pharmacy practice section. This type of prescribing is not addressed by the DEA, but individual state medical boards and boards of pharmacy can prohibit treating oneself or immediate family members. Some states prohibit prescribing certain categories of drugs to oneself or to family members, such as schedule II drugs or all controlled drugs.

My state sets limits on prescribing controlled drugs to oneself or family members. Yes / No

If yes, list the limitations on prescribing to oneself or to family members in your state:

Checking the Validity of a DEA Number

Each DEA number is unique and is assigned to an individual healthcare provider or to an institution. The DEA number permits the individual to write for controlled substances, and permits the institution to order and manage controlled substances. DEA numbers must meet in order to be valid. Each DEA number is randomly-generated and begins with 2 letters, followed by 7 numbers. The last number is called the "check digit". The first letter identifies the type of practitioner or institution:

A/B/F/G – Hospital/clinic/practitioner/teaching institution/pharmacy

M – Mid-level practitioner (nurse practitioners, physician assistants, optometrists, etc.)

P/R – Manufacturer/distributor/researcher/analytical lab/importer/exporter/reverse distributor/narcotic treatment program

The second letter of the DEA number is the first letter of the prescriber's last name. For example: Wendy Clark, MD has the DEA number AC2143799, where A is the initial letter (Dr. Clark is a physician), C is for her last name (Clark), followed by 7 numeric digits.

If a practitioner is authorized to prescribe narcotics (such as buprenorphine) for opioid addiction treatment, the practitioner will receive a second DEA number. The number is the same as the original DEA number, except that the letter "X" replaces the first letter. The provision that permits this prescribing is called "DATA 2000" and is described further in this booklet. If Dr. Clark decided to take this training and could then prescribe for this purpose, her DATA 2000 waiver unique identification number (UIN) would be XC2143799. Both her DEA number and her UIN should be on the prescription.

Prescribers in a hospital or other institution, including medical interns, residents, and visiting physicians, can prescribe medication under the DEA registration of that hospital or institution.

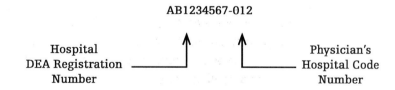

Steps to Verify the Validity of a DEA Number

Step one: Add the 1st, 3rd and 5th digits together.

Step two: Add the 2nd, 4th and 6th digits together.

Step three: Multiply the result of step two by 2.

Step four: Add the results of step one and step three together. The last digit of this sum should match the last digit of the prescriber's DEA number. This is called the check digit.

Example: DEA number BT6835752

Step one: 6 + 3 + 7 = 16
Step two: 8 + 5 + 5 = 18
Step three: 18 x 2 = 36
Step four: 16 + 36 = 52

The last digit of the sum in step four is 2. This should be the same as the last digit of the DEA number. Therefore, this DEA number appears to be valid.

Verify Dr. Mikacich's DEA number (B M 6 1 2 5 3 4 1) by completing the four steps after verifying that the first letter confers the ability to prescribe and the second letter matches the first letter of the last name.

Step one:
Step two:
Step three:
Step four:

The last digit of the sum in step four is _____.

Does Dr. Mikacich's DEA number appear to be valid?*   Yes / No

*Answer: Yes; the number appears to be valid.

Written Prescriptions for Controlled Substances

The prescription for a controlled substance must be written in ink, indelible pencil, or type-written by the prescriber or prepared by an agent of the prescriber (such as an office assistant or nurse). It must be signed and dated by the prescriber.

The prescription must include:

- The patient's full name and address

- The prescriber's full name, business address, and DEA number

- The drug name, strength, dosage form, quantity prescribed and directions for use

- The number of refills authorized

Orders written for direct administration to patients in facilities such as clinics and hospitals are not considered prescriptions (they are referred to as medication orders) and do not need to meet prescription requirements.

Tamper Resistant Security Forms

In order for outpatient drugs to be paid for under the federal Medicaid program, all written prescriptions must be on tamper resistant security forms that contain at least three tamper resistant security features. This does not apply to electronic, oral, or faxed prescriptions.

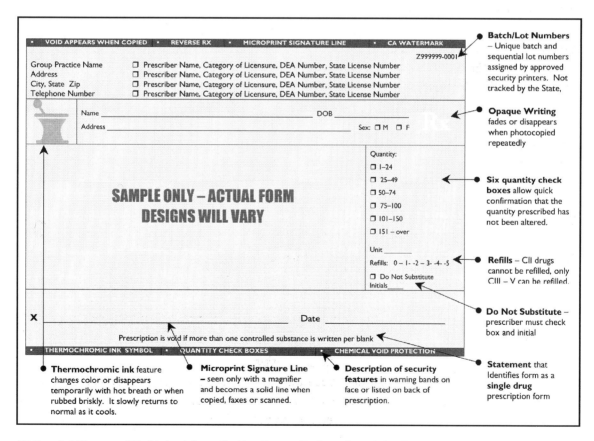

CA Board of Pharmacy "What to Look for on the New Tamper-Resistant Prescription Forms", at http://www.pharmacy.ca.gov/publications/single_rxform.pdf (accessed 2015 Sep 3).

CMS requires security features that include the following:

1.   Prevents duplication (e.g., the word "void" appears due to thermochromic ink, which appears if photocopied)

2.   Prevents the erasure or modification of the written information (e.g., quantity check boxes, refill indicators, or chemically reactive paper)

3.   Prevents the use of counterfeit forms (e.g., pre-printed serial numbers or watermarks)

States can require the use of tamper resistant security forms for all prescriptions, for all scheduled drugs, or for schedule II drugs only. Many states have the same or similar requirements for the security forms. Prescribers can have both security and non-security forms. Some prescribers choose to use security forms for all prescriptions, which is acceptable, but more costly.

My state requires tamper resistant security forms for these categories of drugs (e.g., all drugs, all scheduled drugs only, schedule II drugs only):

_____

If required for certain patient groups, fill in the type of patients:

_____

Describe the security elements that must be present on the form in your state:

_____

Oral (Phone) Prescriptions for Controlled Substances

Pharmacists can receive prescriptions for schedule III, IV, and V drugs over the phone. The pharmacist must reduce the prescription to writing and include all information required on a prescription, with the exception of the prescriber's signature and date. To "reduce the prescription to writing" means to transcribe (write) the oral prescription onto the pharmacy's prescription blank.

Oral prescriptions of schedule II drugs are not valid except in emergency situations. In an emergency, the pharmacist can fill enough to tide the patient over until a prescription can be received. Oral, emergency prescriptions for schedule II drugs are discussed further in this booklet under Emergency Filling.

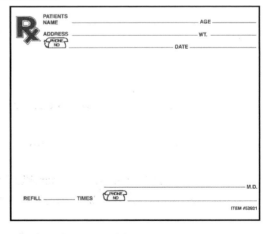

A blank prescription form used in a pharmacy for reducing oral prescriptions to writing

The prescriber can be busy with patients and may not have time to personally call the pharmacy to authorize oral prescriptions. Federal law permits prescribers to designate someone else (such as the office staff or a nurse) to communicate new and refill information to pharmacists by telephone or fax. This person does not need to be licensed or have any special training. The communication must be under the supervision of the prescriber and the prescriber is responsible for their actions and any medication errors that occur due to errors made by the prescriber's staff.

Faxed Prescriptions for Controlled Substances

Faxed prescriptions are acceptable for schedule III-V drugs as long as all information required on a prescription is included, and the prescriber has signed the fax prior to sending it to the pharmacy. Sometimes, a prescriber will write the prescription for a schedule III-V drug on a tamper resistant security form and fax it over to the pharmacy. This is legal, however the security form can contain the text "void" over the face of the prescription due to the effect of the heat from the fax machine on the thermochromic ink. This is a security feature intended to prevent people from creating fake prescriptions or faxing the same prescription to multiple pharmacies. The pharmacist should exercise professional judgment in determining the validity of the prescription and contact the prescriber for verification if there are any doubts.

Generally, faxed prescriptions for schedule II drugs cannot serve as the original prescription. However, some prescribers' offices will fax the prescription to the pharmacy, and provide the patient with the same prescription to bring to the pharmacy. The purpose of faxing the prescription is to permit the pharmacy to begin to process the prescription in order to reduce the patient's wait time. The schedule II drug cannot be dispensed to the patient until the patient gives the written prescription to the pharmacy. The written prescription is then verified against the faxed prescription, prior to dispensing. It is not acceptable for patients to fax the prescription to the pharmacy, even as an alert, although this is done in some settings.

There are three exceptions where a faxed prescription can serve as an original prescription for a schedule II drug

- If the drug is being compounded for administration to a patient by the parenteral, intravenous, intramuscular, subcutaneous, or intraspinal route

- If the medication is going to a resident of a long-term care facility (LTCF)

- If the patient is in a Medicare-certified or state-licensed hospice program. The prescriber must note on the face of the prescription that the prescription is for a hospice patient

The fax can be sent by anyone in the office that has been designated by the prescriber.

Electronic Prescriptions for Controlled Substances

The documentation of medical care in most healthcare settings is conducted electronically. This includes electronic medical records, computer-based prescribing systems, and networks to transmit and receive prescriptions. When prescriptions are electronically transmitted entirely through software, safeguards must be in place to prevent unauthorized persons from hacking into the system and illegally transmitting controlled substance prescriptions. In 2010, the DEA released final rules that permit electronic prescriptions for controlled substances (EPCS) for schedules II-V drugs.

Prescribers and pharmacies are still in the process of implementing e-prescribing. Most prescribers can use EPCS for all schedules and most pharmacies can receive prescriptions for all schedules.

Prescribers and pharmacies must use DEA-approved software that has passed a DEA-sanctioned audit by a third party (outside company) in order to send and receive EPCS. Prescribers must use a 2-factor authentication method to sign and transmit e-prescriptions. 2-factor authentication adds an extra layer of security over one-factor authentication. An example of one-factor authentication is entering a single password to gain access to an email account or online banking account. The credentials that are permitted for DEA-sanctioned validation will include two of the following:[56]

■ Something you know (such as a password or response to a question)

■ Something you have (a hard token, which is a cryptographic key stored on a hardware device kept separately from the computer being accessed, such as a PDA, cell phone, smart card, or flash drive)

■ Something you are (biometric information, such as an iris or fingerprint scan)

Passwords and answers to questions are easily observed, guessed, and hacked. This is why a hard token or biometric information must be used as well. As an alternative to using 2-factor authentication to sign the EPCS, the prescriber can use a digital certificate. A digital certificate contains the user's credentials and is issued by the DEA. Keep in mind that the prescriber's software used to transmit the prescription and the pharmacy's software used to receive the prescription must be DEA-approved.

If the prescriber sends a prescription from software that is pending DEA approval, the pharmacy will need to print out the prescription and contact the prescriber for verification. If the prescriber was contacted by telephone, then the prescription is now considered an oral prescription. If the prescriber was contacted by fax, then the prescription is now considered a faxed prescription (as long as the fax has been manually signed by the prescriber prior to transmission). If the prescriber's software is still pending DEA approval, it cannot be used to transmit prescriptions.

---

56   http://www.deadiversion.usdoj.gov/ecomm/e_rx/faq/practitioners.htm (accessed 2015 Jul 30).

When a prescription is received electronically, federal law requires that the prescription and all required annotations (i.e., prescription corrections) must be stored electronically for at least 2 years, which matches the requirements in most states. Some states have stricter requirements; the longest is Arizona, which requires keeping prescription records for 7 years.

My state requires that paper forms and electronic versions of forms for scheduled drugs (DEA 222 forms/disposal forms/prescriptions/invoices) be kept for this number of years: _____

A prescriber can sign multiple electronic prescriptions for controlled drugs for a single patient with a single digital signature. However, a single signature cannot be used to sign prescriptions for different patients. If a prescriber needs to issue a prescription for a different patient, the prescriber must repeat the process for a new digital signature.

If transmission of an electronic prescription for schedule III-V drugs fails, the prescriber will need to send it to the pharmacy by another method, such as on a paper prescription form, by fax or by phone. If an electronic prescription is not received in a timely manner, it may be due to a lag in the electronic delivery. To make sure that the prescription is not filled twice, the replacement must specify that an initial electronic transmission has failed, with the date, time, and pharmacy where the initial electronic prescription had been sent. The pharmacy will need to verify that the initial electronic prescription was not received or dispensed. If the initial prescription was received and dispensed, then the second prescription is voided. If the initial prescription was received but not dispensed, then the initial prescription is voided and the pharmacy uses the replacement to provide the drug to the patient.

Multiple Prescriptions for Schedule II Drugs

Schedule II drugs can be used to treat chronic conditions such as opioids used for pain or stimulants used for attention deficit hyperactivity disorder. Since refills for schedule II drugs are prohibited under federal law, the patient would need to see the prescriber monthly in order to obtain a new prescription. This can require taking time off from work or school each month for the medical appointments, and can be expensive in terms of transportation and medical co-pays.

In 2007, the DEA provided a work-around to permit patients to receive up to a 90-day supply of schedule II drugs with a single office visit. The prescriber can write for multiple (usually two or three) prescriptions for a schedule II drug which are filled sequentially, and cannot exceed a 90-day supply in total. The prescription cannot be post-dated. The prescriber must include two dates: when the prescription was written, and the earliest acceptable fill date. For example, if the patient was seen on April 1, 2015, the prescriber can provide the patient with three identical prescriptions, each for a 30-day supply of the schedule II drug, and all dated with the issue date of April 1, 2015. The first prescription can be filled on the day it was written (April 1, 2015), the second prescription will include the earliest possible fill date ("do not fill until May 1, 2015") and the third prescription will also include the earliest possible fill date ("do not fill until June 1, 2015"). The prescriber must indicate the "earliest acceptable fill date" in order to prevent the patient from filling more than one prescription at the same time at different pharmacies. The DEA does not place a quantity or time limit from the issue date for dispensing schedule II prescriptions, but some states have specific requirements.

My state sets a time limit on the days/months from the issue date when a schedule II must be filled. If yes, list the permitted time period: Yes / No _____

My state permits patients to receive more than one month's worth of a schedule II drug at one time.   Yes / No

If yes, list if a maximum time period applies:

_____

Pre-signing Prescriptions for Controlled Substances

According to the CSA, a prescription for a controlled substance must be signed and dated on the date it is issued to the patient.

Pre-signing prescriptions for controlled substances is not permitted. Prescribers have pre-signed (and pre-dated) prescription blanks in the past so that staff in their office, such as a nurse who may be seeing patients in the prescriber's absence, can provide prescriptions to the patients. The prescriber would sign and date prescription blanks for the time they are out of the office, and the rest of the prescription would be filled in at a later time with the patient's name, medication, and directions. Pre-signing prescription blanks for non-scheduled and scheduled drugs is illegal and has resulted in disciplinary actions and license suspensions. Pharmacists should not fill prescriptions that are suspected to have been pre-signed.

Errors or Omissions on a Controlled Substance Prescription

In most states, a pharmacist can amend minor misspellings, fill-in the patient's address, and add the prescriber's DEA number to a prescription. The pharmacist can amend the dosage form, strength, quantity and directions for use, after consultation with the prescriber. This includes making any quantity changes required for insurance coverage. All significant changes will need to be documented on the prescription and the pharmacist will write his or her name or initials to indicate who made the call to the prescriber.

For all schedules of controlled substances, there are three items that cannot be changed: the patient's name, the drug itself (except for generic substitution), and the prescriber's signature. If any of the three items above need to be changed, or if the prescriber did not sign the prescription, the prescription is invalid and a new prescription will be required. Minor spelling mistakes in the patient's name or drug name can be corrected at the pharmacist's discretion.

Pharmacists cannot change the drug that is written on the prescription. However, most states permit the pharmacist to substitute a brand name drug with the generic equivalent. Changing the drug entirely would constitute a major error and could be an attempt at drug diversion. For example, *Opana ER* has a much higher street value than generic morphine ER.

It is unlikely that the prescriber misspelled his or her own name, although it may be difficult for the pharmacy staff to decipher the correct spelling. If the prescriber's signature is obviously misspelled, the pharmacist should be wary of forgery.

For errors or omissions on prescriptions for schedules III, IV, and V drugs, the pharmacist can simply call the prescriber, note any authorized modification, and document that the prescriber was contacted.

Schedule II drugs are more susceptible to drug abuse and diversion. Laws regarding amendments on prescriptions for schedules II drugs are generally more stringent than with schedule III-V drugs. The DEA defers the decisions on permitted modifications to schedule II prescriptions to the state boards, and to the pharmacist's professional judgment.

In my state the following changes can be made, at the pharmacist's discretion, to schedule II prescriptions:

_____

In my state the following changes can be made, at the pharmacist's discretion, to schedule III-V prescriptions:

_____

THE PRESCRIBER'S AND PHARMACIST'S CORRESPONDING RESPONSIBILITY

Pharmacists are the last line of defense in preventing controlled substances from getting into the wrong hands. A drug can be scheduled due to risks of addiction, physical dependence, and accidental or intentional drug diversion. Diversion is when a drug has been legally prescribed for a medically-necessary use and is used instead by a different person for a use that is illegal and typically is not medically necessary.

A practitioner can issue valid prescriptions for a legitimate medical purpose only. The condition being treated must be one that the prescriber would be expected to treat. If the pharmacist does not believe that the prescription is for a legitimate medical need, then the pharmacist has the right not to fill it. Any concerns regarding the prescription should be investigated. Both the prescriber and the pharmacist share responsibility to prevent drug diversion.

Recognizing Red Flags to Prevent Drug Diversion

More Americans die from prescription drug abuse than from using street drugs such as heroin and crack cocaine. As part of their professional practice, pharmacists assist in preventing prescription drug abuse and diversion. If appropriate, the pharmacist has the right to tell the patient, "I do not feel comfortable filling this prescription," or "I will not fill this prescription." It is considered a felony offense for a pharmacist to knowingly fill an invalid or fraudulent prescription. The law does not require a pharmacist to dispense a prescription of suspicious origin. The NABP recommends watching for the following red flags:

■ Irregularities on the face of the prescription itself

■ Nervous patient demeanor

■ Age or presentation of patient (e.g., youthful patients seeking chronic pain medications)

■ Multiple patients all with the same residential address

■ Multiple prescribers for the same patient for duplicate therapy

■ Cash payments

■ Frequent requests for early refills

■ Suspicious prescriptions brought in at the busiest time while the patient decides to wait for it to be filled

■ Prescriptions written for an unusually large quantity

■ Prescriptions written for duplicative drug therapy

■ Initial prescriptions written for strong opioids

■ Long distances traveled from the patient's home to the prescriber's office or to the pharmacy

■ Irregularities in the prescriber's qualifications in relation to the type of medication/s prescribed

■ Prescriptions for medications with no logical connection to an illness or condition

- Patients coming to the pharmacy in groups (especially if most of the patients live far away from the pharmacy or prescriber and each patient has similar prescriptions issued by the same prescriber)

- The same diagnosis codes for many patients

- The same combinations of drugs prescribed for multiple patients

Prescription Drug Monitoring Programs

All 50 states have a prescription drug monitoring program (PDMP); Missouri was the last state to pass legislation for a PDMP in 2015. A PMDP is a statewide electronic database that collects designated data on drugs dispensed in the state. The DEA is not involved with the administration of any state PDMP. These are very useful for pharmacists who are unsure whether to fill a prescription because the patient may be getting multiple prescriptions filled at multiple pharmacies ("pharmacy hopping"). Prescribers can also check the PDMP when they suspect the patient is "doctor hopping".

The primary purposes of the PDMP are to support access to legitimate medical use of controlled substances and to identify and deter or prevent drug abuse and diversion.

Depending on the state, data is collected in real-time (Oklahoma), daily (e.g., Arizona, Colorado, North Dakota, Kansas, New York), weekly (California, Nevada, Washington, Florida), or monthly (e.g., Alaska, Pennsylvania). States also have various monitoring authority: the PDMP may collect all drugs (non-controlled and controlled), controlled substances only, schedule II only, schedule II-IV only, or schedule II-V only. The PDMP is housed by a specified statewide regulatory, administrative or law enforcement agency. The agency that collects the prescribing data will make it available to individuals who are authorized under state law to receive the information for purposes of their profession. Some states are able to share their data with out-of-state authorized users.

List the schedules of drugs collected in your state's PDMP:

_____

List the collection period (such as weekly, or monthly):

_____

Which healthcare professionals are authorized to access the PDMP in your state?

_____

REFILLS OF CONTROLLED SUBSTANCES

Controlled Substances Eligible for Refills

There are no refill restrictions for schedule V prescriptions under DEA federal requirements. Some states permit refills of schedule V drugs in a manner similar to non-scheduled drugs.

Schedules III and IV prescriptions may be refilled up to 5 times within 6 months of the date written. After 5 refills or after 6 months, whichever occurs first, a new prescription will be required. The original fill is not counted as a refill. A pharmacy may use one of two systems (paper or electronic) for storage and retrieval of prescription refill information of schedules III and IV drugs.

Refills on schedule II prescriptions are prohibited.

My state has requirements for schedule V drugs refills that are more stringent than refill requirements for non-scheduled drugs. Yes / No

If yes, list them here:

_____

Paper Recordkeeping Requirements for Refills of Schedule III - IV Drugs

There are federal requirements to document each refill of schedules III and IV drugs. The pharmacist must notate on the back of the prescription: his or her initials, the date dispensed, and the amount dispensed. If the amount dispensed is not notated for each refill, it is assumed that the pharmacist dispensed a refill for the remaining amount.

Electronic Recordkeeping Requirements for Refills of Schedule III - IV Drugs

If an electronic recordkeeping system is utilized, the pharmacist must verify and document that the refill data entered into the system is correct. All computer generated prescription and refill documentation must be stored in a separate file at the pharmacy and must be maintained for a period of 2 years from the dispensing date. A state may decide that the records should be kept for a longer period.

Either of the following methods is acceptable:

- A daily, hard copy printout of refills for controlled substances with the signature and date of all the pharmacists involved with the dispensing during that day. This signifies that the pharmacists agree that the printout is correct, and includes what they refilled for the day. Printouts can be long, and may be sent from a central "computer room" location. This is more common in pharmacies that fill a large number of prescriptions. The printout must be provided to the pharmacy within 72 hours of the date on which the refill was dispensed.

- A bound logbook or separate file documenting each day's refills. Each dispensing pharmacist during the day signs a statement saying that what they dispensed is correctly listed in the logbook or file.

The electronic system must provide online retrieval of original prescription information for those prescriptions currently authorized for refill. The information must include:

- Original prescription number

- Date of issuance

- Patient's full name and address

- Prescriber's name, address, and DEA registration number

- The name, strength, dosage form and quantity of the controlled substance prescribed (and quantity dispensed if different from the quantity prescribed)

- Total number of refills authorized by the prescriber

The electronic recordkeeping system must be able to print out refill information, which must include:

- Original prescription number

- Date of each refill

- Patient's name and address

- Prescriber's name

- Name or identification code of the dispensing pharmacist

- Quantity dispensed

Processing Schedule III - IV Refills When the Computer System is Down

Although computers offer an efficient method for managing pharmacy workflow, electronic recordkeeping systems are susceptible to downtime. Downtime occurs when the computer system is not working properly and is unavailable to the pharmacy staff. This can occur due to power outages, system crashes, or scheduled software maintenance. Most pharmacies with software applications and systems will experience downtime.

In the event that the pharmacy's electronic system experiences downtime, the DEA requires pharmacies to develop a back-up procedure to document the dispensing of refills of schedules III and IV drugs. Although not addressed by federal regulations, the pharmacy should also have a back up procedure in place to document the dispensing (new fills and refills) of all other prescriptions. Individual states and stores can require stricter policies.

The DEA is most concerned with schedule III and IV drugs because schedule II drugs do not have refills, and schedule V drugs are less dangerous and have less risk of diversion.

The back-up procedure must ensure that refills have been authorized by the original prescription, and that the maximum number of refills has not been exceeded. The pharmacy will need to be able to provide refills to patients and keep accurate records of refills that were dispensed during downtime. Once the computer system is functioning properly, all the required information needs to be entered into the electronic system as soon as possible.

Since pharmacies are required to maintain a daily record of refills as a printout or bound logbook, refill information should be accessible during system downtime. Federal regulations also mandate that any electronic system employed by a pharmacy must have a central recordkeeping location that can provide a printout of the refill information to the requesting pharmacy within 48 hours. In large hospital centers, there will be a central data location that prints out dispensing records on a regular basis.

The prescription itself can be prepared using a tabletop label printer if the power is down entirely, or with hand-written labels. The pharmacist must use caution that all required information is documented during system downtime.

PARTIAL FILLING OF CONTROLLED SUBSTANCES

Partial Fills of Schedule III-V Prescriptions

Partial refills of schedule III, IV, and V drugs are permitted by the DEA if it is recorded in the same manner as a refill and if the total quantity dispensed in all of the fills does not exceed the total quantity prescribed. No dispensing can occur beyond 6 months past the date of issue. Partial fills are not considered refills. For example, a prescription for *Ultram* #60 with 2 refills is equivalent to 180 tablets to be dispensed over a 6-month period from the date of issue. Theoretically, the patient can come into the pharmacy every day for 90 days and receive two tablets, or come in daily for 180 days for one tablet.

Partial Fills of Schedule II Prescriptions

Partial filling of schedule II prescriptions, either written or electronically sent to the pharmacy, are permissible if:

- The pharmacy does not have sufficient stock of the drug

- The pharmacist needs additional time to verify the legitimacy of the prescription

- The patient requests a lesser quantity, which is commonly due to the cost of the drug

When a pharmacist fills less than the full amount on the prescription, he or she notes on the prescription the amount filled and must fill the remainder within 72 hours, or the remainder is void and the prescriber must be notified. If medically necessary, the prescriber can decide to issue a new prescription for the remaining amount.

It is common for pharmacies to partially fill controlled substance prescriptions for terminally ill patients or LTCF residents in order to reduce drug diversion and waste that can occur if the patient expires before the medications are finished. "Terminally ill" is often used in hospice settings to indicate that the patient is expected to have less than 6 months to live. These prescriptions are often written for schedule II opioids, which are used to relieve severe pain during the patient's remaining days.

The reason for the partial fill must be noted on the prescription, such as "terminally ill" or "LTCF resident." The pharmacist has much longer than the typical 72 hours to fill the remainder. For terminally ill patients or LTCF residents, the pharmacist can partially fill prescriptions in increments for up to 60 days from the date the prescription was written. For each partial fill, the pharmacist must indicate:

- Date of partial filling

- Amount dispensed

- Amount remaining

- Name of dispensing pharmacist

If an electronic recordkeeping system is used, the following information must be maintained and be updated in real-time when a partial fill is dispensed:

■ Original prescription number

■ Date of issue

■ Prescriber's name

■ Patient's name

■ Address of LTCF, hospital, or patient's home

■ Drug name, dose, formulation, strength, and quantity

■ Quantity authorized

■ List of partial fills dispensed

EMERGENCY FILLING OF CONTROLLED SUBSTANCES

Emergency Filling of Schedule III-V Drugs without Prescriber's Authorization

As discussed in the pharmacy practice section, some states allow emergency refills without the prescriber's authorization if the prescriber is unavailable to authorize the refill and, if in the pharmacist's professional judgment, failure to refill the prescription might interrupt the patient's ongoing care and have a significant adverse effect on the patient's well-being. The pharmacist must make a reasonable effort to contact the prescriber.

Limitations on emergency filling without the prescriber's authorization will vary from state-to-state. Some states allow emergency filling for non-scheduled drugs and schedule III-V drugs. Other states only allow emergency refilling of non-scheduled drugs. The emergency days supply to be dispensed varies by state - this is typically 72 hours but can be up to a one-month supply. The emergency refill must be properly documented and an original prescription for the emergency filling must be obtained in a timely manner.

In contrast, federal law prohibits emergency fills of schedule II medications without a prescriber's authorization. Emergency fills of schedule II drugs will require the prescriber's oral authorization at a minimum.

My state allows emergency filling of non-controlled drugs without the prescriber's authorization. Yes / No

My state allows emergency filling of schedule III-V drugs without the prescriber's authorization. Yes / No

My state allows an emergency filling of up to _____ days supply.

My state has further limitations on emergency filling without the prescriber's authorization (such as receiving a new prescription within a designated time period). Yes / No

If yes, list the limitations:

Emergency Filling of Schedule II Drugs

In normal circumstances, prescribers cannot call in prescriptions for schedule II drugs; these must be authorized as a written or electronic prescription. However, the DEA permits emergency dispensing of orally authorized prescriptions for schedule II drugs if the immediate administration of the drug is necessary to avoid patient harm and if there is no reasonable alternative. Electronic prescriptions provide an immediate method to transmit an original prescription to the pharmacy, but an orally authorized prescription can still be needed if the prescriber's or pharmacy's EPCS system experiences downtime, if such a system is not present, or if the prescriber is away from the office.

If the pharmacist is not familiar with the prescriber, the pharmacist must make a reasonable effort to determine that the oral authorization came from a DEA registered practitioner, which can include a call back to the prescriber using the telephone number listed in a public directory (i.e., not the number on the prescription form since this may be a fake) and/or other good faith efforts to ensure the prescriber's identity. The prescription must be reduced to writing immediately by the pharmacist and must contain all the necessary information except for the prescriber signature. The quantity dispensed should be the minimum necessary amount until a prescription can be written or electronically transmitted. This amount is up to the pharmacist's professional judgment.

The prescriber must provide an original prescription (written or electronic) by the 7th day following the fill date. The written prescription can be hand-delivered or mailed and postmarked by the 7th day. The written prescription needs to include the statement "Authorization for Emergency Dispensing" on the face and the date of the oral prescription. Once received, the pharmacist must attach the written prescription to the emergency oral prescription. For electronic prescriptions, the pharmacist must annotate the record of the electronic prescription with the emergency authorization and the date of the oral order. If the original prescription is not received, the pharmacist must report the breach to the local DEA office.

Central fill pharmacies are prohibited from preparing emergency fills for schedule II drugs, even if receiving an oral request from a prescriber.

My state has additional limitations on emergency filling of schedule II drugs. Yes / No

If yes, list the requirements:

_____

LABEL REQUIREMENTS FOR CONTROLLED SUBSTANCES

Labeling Requirements for All Controlled Substances
Each prescription dispensed must include the following items on the container:

- Date of initial fill

- Date of current fill for schedule III-V refills (schedule II prescriptions have no refills, therefore, the initial fill date will be the only date on the label)

- Pharmacy name and address

- Prescription serial number

- Name of patient

- Name of prescriber

- Directions for use

- Cautionary statements

- Refills (if any)

Additional Label Requirement for Central Fill Pharmacies

If the prescription is filled at a central fill pharmacy, the central fill pharmacy must include the retail pharmacy's name and address on the label, and a unique identifier (such as the central fill pharmacy's DEA number) to indicate that it was centrally filled.

DEA-Required Warning Statement on Label

Schedule II, III and IV drugs are required to have the following warning on the container when dispensed: "CAUTION: Federal law prohibits the transfer of this drug to any person other than the person for whom it was prescribed." Schedule V drugs are not required to have this statement affixed to the label.

Exemptions to Labeling Requirements

The labeling requirements are not required with an inpatient medication (ordered with a "medication order") and if the drug will be administered by a healthcare professional. The use must be short-term; schedule II drugs can be for a maximum 7-day period, and schedules III, IV and V drugs can be for a maximum period of no more than a 34-day supply or 100 dosage units (whichever is less). The institution must have appropriate safeguards in place for the safe distribution of controlled substances.

TRANSFERRING CONTROLLED SUBSTANCE PRESCRIPTIONS

Transferring Schedule III-V Prescriptions

Schedule III, IV and V drugs are only allowed one transfer that must be by direct communication between two licensed pharmacists (or certified pharmacy technicians, in states that permit this practice). The only exception is if the pharmacies share a real-time, online database of the prescription database (such as stores in the same chain). With this type of shared prescription database, different pharmacies can transfer up to the maximum number of refills on the prescription.

For the transferring pharmacy, the prescription hard copy is pulled and "void" is written on the face (front). The following information of the receiving pharmacy is written on the back of the voided prescription:

- Pharmacy's name

- Business address

- DEA number

- Name of transferring pharmacist

- Name of receiving pharmacist

■ Date of transfer

For the receiving pharmacy, the prescription is reduced to writing by the pharmacist and "transfer" is written on the face of the transferred prescription. The following information must be recorded:

■ Date the original prescription was issued

■ Original number of refills

■ Date it was first dispensed

■ Number of refills remaining

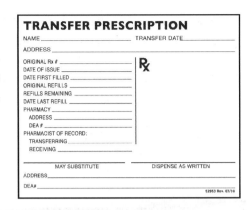

Transfer form for receiving a prescription from another pharmacy.

■ Pharmacy's name, business address, DEA registration number, and prescription number from which the prescription information was transferred

■ Name of pharmacist who transferred the prescription

■ Pharmacy's name, business address, DEA registration number, and prescription number from which the prescription was originally filled

Alternatively, the above information may be documented electronically. Records must be kept for 2 years, according to federal law; a state can set a longer requirement.

Transferring Schedule II Prescriptions

Schedule II prescriptions cannot be transferred from one pharmacy to another for the purpose of dispensing to a patient.

If a pharmacy does not have a schedule II drug in stock and has received a written prescription for the drug, the pharmacy can return the prescription to the patient and instruct the patient to have it filled at a different store if the patient needs the prescription filled the same day. If it is an electronic prescription, the patient should contact the prescriber to send the electronic prescription to another pharmacy.

If the pharmacy has enough drug in stock for a partial fill, the pharmacy can fill a partial, order more from the drug wholesaler, and have the patient return for the remaining amount within 72 hours. Another solution is for the pharmacy to borrow or purchase the schedule II drug from a nearby pharmacy, which will require a Form 222.

PATIENT IDENTIFICATION PRIOR TO DISPENSING CONTROLLED SUBSTANCES

Is the person picking up the medication the actual patient that the medication has been prescribed to, or is it a person pretending to be the patient?

There are instances of drug diversion where a person comes to the pharmacy and falsely claims another patient's controlled substance by providing another patient's name or claiming to be the designated caregiver. The federal government, as part of a recent initiative to reduce drug diversion, has recommended that pharmacies require identification prior to dispensing a controlled substance if the patient is not known to the pharmacy staff. There is presently no federal law requiring patients to provide identification prior to receiving prescriptions. Many states require identification.

The most commonly used identifiers are the patient's name and date of birth. If the patient has a common name, the home address can be requested for additional verification. Some states require patient identification for all prescriptions in the community setting while other states require identification only for controlled substances.

Some states will require pharmacies to submit a patient's identification number to the state prescription drug monitoring program to monitor and prevent drug diversion. The identification number is defined as the unique number contained in the state-issued valid driver's license, a valid military identification card, a valid identification card issued by the bureau of motor vehicles, or an assigned unique identification number that could be linked to other personal identifiers. In states where identification is not required, it can be requested at the discretion of the pharmacist or in "red flag" circumstances.

My state requires patients to present identification when picking up all prescriptions. Yes / No

My state requires patients to present identification when picking up controlled substance prescriptions only. Yes / No

If there are specific identification requirements different than discussed above, list them:

_____

DISPENSING NON-PRESCRIPTION CONTROLLED SUBSTANCES

Some of the schedule V drugs or codeine-containing cough syrups (e.g., *Cheratussin AC*) are not considered prescription drugs, as defined by the FDA. These drugs do not meet the criteria for toxicity potential or require prescriber supervision, as outlined in the Durham-Humphrey Amendment. Therefore, some states permit the pharmacist to sell select controlled substances directly to patients without a prescription, with certain restrictions. Many states and individual stores have elected to keep these controlled substances behind the counter. Other states have stricter rules and require prescriptions for all scheduled drugs, including all schedule V drugs.

My state permits pharmacists to sell select schedule V cough syrups without a prescription.
Yes / No

If there are requirements under which these can be sold, list them:

_____

Opium and codeine can be contained in these products, and these can be abused if taken in excessive amounts. For this reason, there are federal maximum limits on the amount of drug that can be dispensed every 2 days:

- 240 mL (8 ounces) or 48 dosage units of any controlled substance containing opium

- 120 mL (4 ounces) or 24 dosage units of any other controlled substance

Only the pharmacist can dispense a nonprescription controlled substance to a patient, who must be at least 18 years of age. If the pharmacist does not know the patient, the patient must provide proper identification. The pharmacist has to record the following information in a bound record book: the patient's name and address, the drug name and quantity purchased, the date of each purchase, and the pharmacist's name or initials. After the pharmacist dispenses the drug, the payment and delivery may be completed by a non-pharmacist staff member.

DELIVERING CONTROLLED SUBSTANCES TO PATIENTS

The U.S. Postal Services regulations permit pharmacies to deliver controlled substances to patients if the pharmacy is registered or exempt with the DEA. Most of the private common carriers, including FedEx, permit the same. The following preparation and packaging standards must be met:

- The prescription label contains the name and address of the pharmacy (or practitioner) dispensing the prescription

- The inner container is marked and sealed as required by the CSA, and is placed in a plain outer container or securely wrapped in plain paper

- The outside wrapper or container is free of markings that could indicate the contents

COMPOUNDING OR REPACKAGING CONTROLLED SUBSTANCES

A pharmacy may compound schedule II-V drugs for a prescriber's office use under these circumstances:

- It is compounded as an aqueous, oleaginous, or solid dosage form

- It does not contain > 20% controlled substances *(Ex. Ketamine 10%)*

- It is only distributed to prescribers authorized to dispense controlled substances

DISPENSING CONTROLLED SUBSTANCES IN LONG-TERM CARE FACILITIES

Partial Filling of Schedule II Drugs for LTCF Patients

It is common for outpatient pharmacies to partially fill controlled substance prescriptions for LTCF residents and the terminally ill in order to reduce drug diversion and waste that can occur if the patient expires before the medications are finished. The pharmacist has much longer than the typical 72 hours to fill the remainder. For terminally ill patients or LTCF residents, the pharmacist can partially fill prescriptions in increments for up to 60 days from the date the prescription was written.

Automated Dispensing Systems in LTCFs

The DEA permits retail pharmacies to install and remotely operate automated dispensing systems (ADS) in LTCFs. An ADS can also be called an automated dispensing cabinet (ADC).

The ADS electronically records and dispenses single doses of medication. The pharmacist must enter the prescription information into the system before a medication is dispensed from the ADS, with the exception of emergency overrides (which should be strictly limited).

Retrieving drugs from an ADS

The drugs stocked in the ADS are considered pharmacy stock (not LTCF stock) before they are dispensed. The pharmacy must have a separate DEA registration for the ADS located at the LTCF. Only authorized LTCF staff members are allowed access to the ADS. The purpose of utilizing the ADS is to reduce waste of controlled substances, which happens because patients passed away, have been discharged, or had a change of medication. Using the ADS is also more convenient and less labor intensive than preparing daily medication cassettes for each patient.

Emergency Kits for LTCFs

Patients can check into a LTCF outside of regular business hours or need medication for an acute purpose that is not on their regular medication plan. It takes time for pharmacies that are not on-site (physically located at the LTCF) to receive the prescription, enter in the order, and deliver it to the facility. For this reason, the DEA permits controlled substances to be included with the emergency kit at the LTCF. The DEA requires that the controlled substances comes from a DEA registrant and that security safeguards are in place to restrict access. When a medication has been given to a patient, the prescriber should write a prescription for the use and a pharmacist will enter it into the system to document the use of the drug.

INTERNET PHARMACIES AND THE RYAN HAIGHT AMENDMENTS

There are generally two types of Internet pharmacies: legitimate mail order pharmacies and rogue Internet pharmacies. Legitimate mail order pharmacies dispense medications only with a prescription from a prescriber who has performed a good faith medical exam, while rogue pharmacies do not. In 2008, the Ryan Haight Online Pharmacy Consumer Protection Act was signed into law to regulate Internet pharmacies that sell controlled substances.

The following requirements should be met in order to sell controlled substances online:

- Registration with the DEA as a pharmacy and completion of the *Application for Modification for Online Pharmacies.*

- Notifying the DEA and state boards of pharmacy in each state in which it intends to conduct business 30 days before dispensing through the Internet.

- Displaying on the homepage a declaration stating the following: *"In accordance with the Controlled Substances Act and the DEA regulations, this online pharmacy has made the notifications to the DEA Administrator required by 21 U.S.C. § 831 and 21 C.F.R. § 1304.40."*

- The site has to list the physical location of the pharmacy, the contact information (email and phone) and the healthcare professionals employed by the site, including all contracted practitioners, with the degrees and license numbers. The name and license number of the pharmacist-in-charge must be included.

- This statement must be listed on the site and followed: *"This online pharmacy is obligated to comply fully with the Controlled Substances Act and DEA regulations. As part of this obligation, this online pharmacy has obtained a modified DEA registration authorizing it to operate as an online pharmacy. In addition, this online pharmacy will only dispense a controlled substance to a person who has a valid prescription issued for a legitimate medical purpose based upon a medical relationship with a prescribing practitioner. This includes at least one prior in-person medical evaluation in accordance with section 309 of the Controlled Substances Act (21 U.S.C. § 829), or a medical evaluation via telemedicine in accordance with section 102(54) of the Controlled Substances Act (21 U.S.C. § 802(54))."*

- The DEA requires a monthly report of the total quantity of each controlled substance dispensed if over 100 prescriptions have been filled or if 5000 or more dosage units have been filled of all controlled substances.

TREATMENT OF NARCOTIC DEPENDENCE

Addiction, Dependence and Tolerance

Benzodiazepines, barbiturates, opioids, and partial-opioid agonists have three common concerns: addiction, physical or physiological dependence, and tolerance. The National Institute on Drug Abuse defines addiction as a chronic, relapsing brain disease that is characterized by compulsive drug seeking and use, despite harmful consequences. Addiction is a strong need to use a drug for a purpose other than the intended use.

Opioid Treatment Programs

It is estimated that ~ 1 million people in the United States are addicted to heroin and other opioids, including prescription drugs such as oxycodone, hydromorphone and hydrocodone.[57] Patients with this type of addiction are more likely to be co-infected with HIV, hepatitis and sexually transmitted infections. Mental health problems are common among patients with addiction. Criminal histories often stem from the addiction. Treating addiction saves lives, helps families, and reduces healthcare costs.

Methadone blocks the euphoric effects of opioids and helps relieve the craving for the drug of abuse. Methadone is used to treat pain and opioid addiction. Methadone comes in 5, 10 and 40 mg tablets. The 40 mg dose is only indicated for opioid addiction; the lower doses are indicated for pain and opioid addiction. A roadblock for many patients is access to a methadone treatment clinic.

The ability to obtain treatment for opioid addiction improved when the DATA 2000 federal legislation was passed. DATA 2000 permits practitioners to prescribe and dispense schedule III, IV, or V drugs to treat opioid addiction outside of a methadone treatment clinic. Currently, only formulations of buprenorphine with or without naloxone are approved for this purpose (*Suboxone* and *Subutex*).

DATA 2000 requires practitioner training. Once this is completed, the practitioner is referred to as a "DATA waived practitioner" and is given a DATA 2000 waiver unique identification number (UIN). The number is the same as their original DEA number except that the letter "X" replaces the first letter. For example, if Dr. Wendy Clark's DEA number is AC2143799, her UIN would be XC2143799. The UIN is in addition to a prescriber's DEA number and both numbers should be on prescriptions. DATA waived practitioners can treat up to 30 patients at any one time for the first year. After the first year, they can request to increase the limit to treating 100 patients at any one time.

A practitioner who is not specifically registered with the DEA to treat narcotic addiction may administer (but not prescribe) a day's worth of treatment at one time to a patient while the proper referral to an opioid treatment program is being arranged. This can be done for up to 3 days.

57   http://www.cdc.gov/drugoverdose/pdf/hhs_prescription_drug_abuse_report_09.2013.pdf (accessed 2015 Aug 16).

DISTRIBUTION OF CONTROLLED SUBSTANCES BETWEEN DEA REGISTRANTS

A DEA Form 222, or its electronic equivalent, must be used to distribute schedule I and II drugs. An invoice is used to distribute schedule III, IV, and V drugs, which must contain the following information: drug name, dosage form, strength, quantity, date transferred, and recipient's information (name, address, DEA registration number). All records of these transfers (inventory, Form 222, invoice) are kept for at least 2 years, and some states may require paperwork to be maintained for longer than 2 years.

Pharmacy Going Out of Business

If a pharmacy goes out of business or is acquired by new ownership, the pharmacy can transfer the controlled substances to the new pharmacy, once the DEA number is confirmed. A complete inventory must be taken that will be used as the final inventory of the registrant who is going out of business and who is transferring the controlled substances. It is also used as the initial inventory for the registrant acquiring the controlled substances. A copy of the inventory must be included in the records of each pharmacy. The inventory report is not sent to the DEA. This inventory must be taken before the dispensing for the day has started, or at the end of the day, in order to avoid controlled substances being pulled from stock during the time the inventory is being taken.

A pharmacy can also transfer controlled substances to the original supplier, manufacturer, or reverse distributor for disposal.

Pharmacy Selling Controlled Substances

A pharmacy can sell controlled substances to other pharmacies or prescribers (without being registered as a distributor) as long as the total number of dosage units does not exceed 5% of the total number of controlled substances dosage units dispensed per calendar year. Both parties must be registered with the DEA to dispense controlled substances.

DISPOSAL OF CONTROLLED SUBSTANCES

Registrants Returning Controlled Substances to the Wholesaler

Pharmacies can return controlled substances to the drug wholesaler. The pharmacist must maintain a written record showing:

1.   The date of the transaction.

2.   The name, strength, dosage form, and quantity of the controlled substance.

3.   The supplier or manufacturer's name, address, and registration number.

A Form 222 or its electronic equivalent must accompany the transfer of schedule II drugs. The wholesaler will keep Copy 3, and send Copies 1 and 2 to the pharmacy, which is acting as the "supplier". The pharmacy will forward Copy 2 to the DEA.

Returning drugs to wholesalers is discussed further under the pharmacy practice section.

OMB APPROVAL NO. 1117-0007   Expiration Date 9/30/2017

U. S. DEPARTMENT OF JUSTICE – DRUG ENFORCEMENT ADMINISTRATION
REGISTRANT RECORD OF CONTROLLED SUBSTANCES DESTROYED
FORM DEA-41

A. REGISTRANT INFORMATION

Registered Name: DEA Registration Number:

Registered Address:

City: State: Zip Code:

Telephone Number: Contact Name:

B. ITEM DESTROYED
1. Inventory

	National Drug Code or DEA Controlled Substances Code Number	Batch Number	Name of Substance	Strength	Form	Pkg. Qty.	Number of Full Pkgs.	Partial Pkg. Count	Total Destroyed
Examples	16590-598-60	N/A	Kadian	60mg	Capsules	60	2	0	120 Capsules
	0555-0767-02	N/A	Adderall	5mg	Tablet	100	0	83	83 Tablets
	9050	B02120312	Codeine	N/A	Bulk	1.25 kg	N/A	N/A	1.25 kg
1.									
2.									
3.									
4.									
5.									
6.									
7.									

2. Collected Substances

	Returned Mail-Back Package	Sealed Inner Liner	Unique Identification Number	Size of Sealed Inner Liner	Quantity of Packages(s)/Liner(s) Destroyed
Examples	X		MBP1106, MBP1108 - MBP1110, MBP112	N/A	5
		X	CRL1007 - CRL1027	15 gallon	21
		X	CRL1201	5 gallon	1
1.					
2.					
3.					
4.					
5.					
6.					
7.					

Form DEA-41   *See instructions on reverse (page 2) of form.*

DEA Form 41

Registrants Sending Controlled Substances to a Reverse Distributor

A pharmacy can transfer controlled substances to a DEA registered reverse distributor, a company that handles the returns and disposals of scheduled and non-scheduled drugs. In order to handle scheduled drugs, the company will require DEA registration. In no case should drugs be sent to the DEA unless the registrant has received prior approval from the local DEA field office.

When a pharmacy transfers schedule II drugs to a reverse distributor for destruction, the reverse distributor must issue the Form 222 or the electronic equivalent to the pharmacy. The reverse distributor will keep Copy 3, and send Copies 1 and 2 to the pharmacy, which is acting as the "supplier". The pharmacy will forward Copy 2 to the DEA. When schedules III-V drugs are transferred to a reverse distributor for destruction, the pharmacy must maintain a record of distribution that lists the drug name, dosage form, strength, quantity, and date transferred.

The DEA registered reverse distributor who will destroy the controlled substances is responsible for submitting a DEA Form 41 to the DEA when the controlled substances have been destroyed.[58]

Patients Disposing of Controlled Substances

According to the DEA, most illicitly used controlled substances are obtained from the home medicine cabinet of family and friends. More Americans currently abuse prescription drugs than the number of those using cocaine, hallucinogens, heroin, and inhalants combined, according to the 2010 National Survey on Drug Use and Health.[59] The CSA did not provide a legal method for patients to dispose of unwanted controlled drugs, except to return them to law enforcement. Most patients would flush unused medication down the toilet, throw it in the trash, or keep them in the medicine cabinet. In 2010, the DEA provided consumers a safe way to dispose of unused controlled substances by implementing the National Prescription Drug Take Back Day program at over 3,000 collection sites nationwide. The DEA planned on discontinuing the National Prescription Drug Take Back Days in 2014, but decided to reinstate it in 2015.

As of October 2014, the Secure and Responsible Drug Disposal Act allows manufacturers, distributors, reverse distributors, narcotic treatment programs, hospitals/clinics with an on-site pharmacy, and retail pharmacies to register with the DEA to collect controlled drugs from patients. An authorized collector can collect controlled and non-controlled substances, which can be co-mingled in a single collection receptacle. Authorized hospitals, clinics and retail pharmacies can voluntarily maintain collection receptacles at long-term care facilities. These collection receptacles are to collect unused/unwanted drugs from patients only.

---

58   *The DEA Form Registrant Record of Controlled Substances Destroyed is available at:* http://www.deadiversion.usdoj.gov/21cfr_reports/surrend/41_form.pdf *(accessed 2015 Aug 5).*

59   *https://nsduhweb.rti.org/respweb/homepage.cfm (accessed 2015 Aug 2).*

Pharmacies and hospitals cannot dispose of unused/unwanted controlled substances in their inventory or stock in the collection receptacle.[60] This is a welcome change since patients will have more disposal options and do not need to wait for a specific Take Back Day to dispose of their unused medications.

Authorized collectors can also provide mail back packages that patients can use to return controlled substances back to the authorized collector. Pharmacies who want to sell or provide these mail-back packages can partner with an authorized collector.

Patients can also contact their city or county government's household trash and recycling service to see if a local drug collection program is available.

There are now a variety of legal ways to dispose of controlled substances through authorized collection sites, mail back packages, local government drug collection programs, and DEA-sponsored Take Back Days. See the Disposal of Prescription Drugs chapter in the RxPrep Course Book and the pharmacy practice section of this booklet for further discussion on the disposal of prescription drugs.

Disposal of Controlled Substance Wastage in an Institutional Setting

A controlled substance dispensed for immediate administration based on an order in a hospital or other institutional setting remains under the control of that institution, even if the substance is not fully used (such as 3 mL of morphine 1 mg/mL injection solution remaining in a vial that has been labeled for a patient, who no longer needs the drug). The remainder cannot be used any further, and is referred to as "drug wastage" or "pharmaceutical wastage". Drug wastage is not reported with a DEA 41, but it must be properly recorded in a log book.

Controlled Substance Loss or Theft

The DEA requires registrants to report significant losses and all thefts of controlled substances to the local DEA office in writing using DEA Form 106 within 1 business day upon discovery.[61] The individual state board can require report of theft within a certain time period as well. Although not required by federal law, the pharmacy should also report any significant losses of controlled substances to the local law enforcement if theft is suspected. The following considerations are used to determine if the loss is significant:

- If the drugs could be subject to diversion

- The specific substances lost or stolen

- The quantity lost in relation to the type of business

---

60 Updated information on drug disposal can be found on the DEA website: http://www.deadiversion.usdoj.gov/drug_disposal/ (accessed 2015 Aug 2).
61 The DEA Form 106, Report of Theft or Loss of Controlled Substances, is available at: http://www.deadiversion.usdoj.gov/21cfr_reports/theft/ (accessed 2015 Aug 5).

- The individuals with access to the lost or stolen drug

- History or pattern of losses or local diversion issues

- Any unique circumstances surrounding the loss or theft

Unsure if the loss is significant? Report it. If the DEA or state inspector performs an investigation and determines the loss was significant, the store and pharmacy staff will face repercussions. Pharmacists have lost their licenses due to unreported controlled substance loss.

The state board of pharmacy may require notification of the loss, and law enforcement may be involved if theft is suspected or known.

My state requires reporting controlled substance loss or theft within this time period:

_____

Reporting In-Transit Losses of Controlled Substances

The DEA Form 106 is also used to report in-transit losses of controlled substances, which is the responsibility of the wholesaler/distributor who is shipping the drugs to the pharmacy. However, if the pharmacy has signed for the delivery and subsequently notices that some or all of the controlled substances are missing, the pharmacy will be responsible for reporting the loss (which may be theft) of the drugs.

When a central fill pharmacy contracts with carriers to transport filled prescriptions to a retail pharmacy, the central fill pharmacy is responsible for reporting the in-transit loss upon discovery of the loss with Form 106. Alternatively, when a retail pharmacy contracts with carriers to retrieve filled prescriptions from a central fill pharmacy, the retail pharmacy is responsible for reporting in-transit losses upon discovery with Form 106.

REPORT OF THEFT OR LOSS OF CONTROLLED SUBSTANCES

Federal Regulations require registrants to submit a detailed report of any theft or loss of Controlled Substances to the Drug Enforcement Administration.

Complete the front and back of this form in triplicate. Forward the original and duplicate copies to the nearest DEA Office. Retain the triplicate copy for your records. Some states may also require a copy of this report.

OMB APPROVAL
No. 1117-0001

1. Name and Address of Registrant (include ZIP Code)

ZIP CODE

2. Phone No. (Include Area Code)

3. DEA Registration Number

2 ltr. prefix   7 digit suffix

4. Date of Theft or Loss

5. Principal Business of Registrant (Check one)

1 ☐ Pharmacy   5 ☐ Distributor
2 ☐ Practitioner   6 ☐ Methadone Program
3 ☐ Manufacturer   7 ☐ Other (Specify)
4 ☐ Hospital/Clinic

6. County in which Registrant is located

7. Was Theft reported to Police? ☐ Yes ☐ No

8. Name and Telephone Number of Police Department (Include Area Code)

9. Number of Thefts or Losses Registrant has experienced in the past 24 months

10. Type of Theft or Loss (Check one and complete items below as appropriate)

1 ☐ Night break-in   3 ☐ Employee pilferage   5 ☐ Other (Explain)
2 ☐ Armed robbery   4 ☐ Customer theft   6 ☐ Lost in transit (Complete Item 14)

11. If Armed Robbery, was anyone:
Killed? ☐ No ☐ Yes (How many) _____
Injured? ☐ No ☐ Yes (How many) _____

12. Purchase value to registrant of Controlled Substances taken? $

13. Were any pharmaceuticals or merchandise taken? ☐ No ☐ Yes (Est. Value) $

14. IF LOST IN TRANSIT, COMPLETE THE FOLLOWING:

A. Name of Common Carrier

B. Name of Consignee

C. Consignee's DEA Registration Number

D. Was the carton received by the customer? ☐ Yes ☐ No

E. If received, did it appear to be tampered with? ☐ Yes ☐ No

F. Have you experienced losses in transit from this same carrier in the past? ☐ No ☐ Yes (How Many) _____

15. What identifying marks, symbols, or price codes were on the labels of these containers that would assist in identifying the products?

16. If Official Controlled Substance Order Forms (DEA-222) were stolen, give numbers.

17. What security measures have been taken to prevent future thefts or losses?

PRIVACY ACT INFORMATION

AUTHORITY: Section 301 of the Controlled Substances Act of 1970 (PL 91-513).
PURPOSE: Report theft or loss of Controlled Substances.
ROUTINE USES: The Controlled Substances Act authorizes the production of special reports required for statistical and analytical purposes. Disclosures of information from this system are made to the following categories of users for the purposes stated:
A. Other Federal law enforcement and regulatory agencies for law enforcement and regulatory purposes.
B. State and local law enforcement and regulatory agencies for law enforcement and regulatory purposes.
EFFECT: Failure to report theft or loss of controlled substances may result in penalties under Section 402 and 403 of the Controlled Substances Act.

In accordance with the Paperwork Reduction Act of 1995, no person is required to respond to a collection of information unless it displays a ly valid OMB control number. The valid OMB control number for this collection of information is 1117-0001. Public reporting burden for this collection of information is estimated to average 30 minutes per response, including the time for reviewing instructions, searching existing data sources, gathering and maintaining the data needed, and completing and reviewing the collection of information.

FORM DEA - 106 (11-00) Previous editions obsolete

CONTINUE ON REVERSE

DEA Form 106

RECORDKEEPING OF CONTROLLED SUBSTANCES

Every pharmacy must maintain current, complete, and accurate records of each controlled substance purchased, received, stored, distributed, dispensed, or disposed. The DEA requires all records of controlled substances be kept for 2 years, and individual states can have longer requirements. The records that must be kept by a pharmacy include:

- Completed and blank DEA Form 222 or CSOS equivalents

- Power of attorney forms

- Receipts and/or invoices for schedule III, IV, and V drugs

- Initial and biennial inventory records for controlled substances

- Records of transfers of controlled substances between pharmacies

- Records of controlled substances distributed (e.g., sales to other registrants, returns to vendors, distributions to reverse distributors)

- Records of controlled substances dispensed (e.g., prescriptions, schedule V logbook)

- Reports of theft or significant loss (DEA Form 106)

- Inventory of drugs surrendered for disposal (DEA Form 41)

- DEA registration certificate

- Self-certification certificate and paper/electronic logbook for pseudoephedrine sales

Original prescriptions, executed 222 forms and inventory records must be kept at the pharmacy location. Shipping and financial records are generally not needed with diversion investigations and can be stored at a central location if the pharmacy has submitted a written notification to the local DEA Field Office. Additionally, states may also require pharmacies to request permission to store any of the pharmacy records off-site. Unless the registrant is informed by the DEA that the permission to keep central records is denied, the registrant can begin storing these two records at a central storage location 14 days after DEA receives this notification. Upon request, the pharmacy must provide the DEA with the central records within 48 hours.

All schedule II drug records must be kept separate from all other records.

All records of schedules III, IV, and V drugs must be kept either separately from all other records or stored in such a way that the information required is readily retrievable from other records.

My state permits off-site storage of pharmacy records. Yes / No

If yes, list which records can be stored off-site: _____

My state requires a permit for off-site storage of pharmacy records. Yes / No

If the off-site records are requested by an inspector or a law enforcement officer, in what time period must the pharmacy retrieve the records?_____

Paper Prescription Recordkeeping System

Pharmacies have two options for filing paper prescription records:

Option 1 (three separate files):

- A file for schedule II drugs dispensed.

- A file for schedules III, IV and V drugs dispensed.

- A file for all non-controlled drugs dispensed.

Option 2 (two separate files):

- A file for schedule II drugs dispensed.

- A file for all other drugs dispensed (non-controlled and schedules III, IV and V drugs). If this method is used, a prescription for a schedule III, IV or V drug must be made readily retrievable by stamping a red "C" (that is at least an inch high) on the prescription. The red "C" is waived if the pharmacy has an electronic prescription recordkeeping system, which can identify the controlled drugs by the prescription number.

Electronic Prescription Recordkeeping System

Pharmacies have one option for electronic prescription records: if it is received electronically, the record must be kept electronically. The system must be able to sort by prescriber name, patient name, drug dispensed, and date filled. Federal law requires keeping electronic records for two years, individual states can require longer periods. With the use of the Internet, records can be stored out of the store, such as on an external device as long as they are readily retrievable.

Institutional Medication Records

A medication or chart order is written by a prescriber for immediate administration to a patient in a hospital or other institutional setting. The prescriber enters the medication order, the order is sent to the pharmacy for dispensing, and the nurse directly administers the drug to the patient. The drug is never in the possession of the patient. Medication orders are not considered prescriptions and do not need to meet all the CSA requirements of prescription packaging or labeling. However, the medication orders do need to be readily retrievable (either by being kept physically separate from all other orders or electronically retrievable), and the facility needs to keep records of the drug administration.

DEA Controlled Substances Inventory

Prior to opening a new pharmacy, there must be a complete inventory of all controlled substances. If there is no stock of controlled substances on hand, the registrant needs a record that shows a zero inventory. For regular inventories, the pharmacy needs to record the controlled substances currently on hand (drugs on order or drugs that are being returned are not included in the inventory count). The inventory is taken minimally on a biennial basis (every 2 years). Pharmacies must maintain inventory at each location. The inventory records of schedule II drugs must be kept separate from all other controlled substances. There is no requirement to submit a copy of the inventory to the DEA. The inventory should be taken if a loss is suspected.

Inventory is counted at either the beginning or close of business. This avoids controlled substances being pulled from stock during the time the inventory is being taken, and provides a more accurate count.

The records must be maintained in written, typewritten, or printed format. Inventory taken with a recording device must be reduced to writing promptly. The final form of the record must be on paper and must include:

- Date of the inventory

- If the inventory was taken at the beginning or close of business

- Names of controlled substances

- Dosage forms and strengths

- Number of dosage units or volume in each container

- Number of commercial containers

For sealed, unopened containers of all controlled substances, an exact count is needed. There is no need to open a sealed container to perform a count, since the count is listed on the manufacturer's drug container.

For opened containers of controlled substances:

■ All schedule I and II containers require an exact count

■ Schedule III, IV, and V containers with < 1000 dosage units can be estimated

■ Schedule III, IV, and V containers with > 1000 dosage units require an exact count

If a drug becomes scheduled or changes schedules, pharmacies must inventory the newly scheduled drug on the date the scheduling became effective.

RESTRICTIONS OF PSEUDOEPHEDRINE, EPHEDRINE AND DEXTROMETHORPHAN SALES

Pseudoephedrine and Ephedrine

Psuedoephedrine and ephedrine are often obtained in large amounts to illegally produce methamphetamine. "Meth" is a strong CNS stimulant that is used illicitly. Because of the abuse potential, these two products have restricted distribution under the Combat Methamphetamine Epidemic Act (CMEA), first passed in 2005. The CMEA applies to three compounds (pseudoephedrine, ephedrine, and phenylpropanolamine). Ephedrine and pseudoephedrine are available behind the counter. Phenylpropanolamine is currently not available in the United States. The restrictions include single agent and combination products, such as cough/cold tablets and syrups. Any product containing pseudoephedrine or ephedrine must be kept behind the counter or in a locked cabinet. They often are, but do not need to be, located in the pharmacy as long as the area with the products and logbook is inaccessible to customers.

The only sale that does not require documentation is the purchase of a single dose packet of pseudoephedrine that contains a maximum of 60 mg (two of the 30 mg tablets). This exception does not apply to ephedrine. For any pseudoephedrine sale greater than 60 mg, and all ephedrine sales, the customer must show photo identification issued by a state (e.g., driver's license, identification card) or from the federal government (e.g., passport).

Purchasers are limited by law to a maximum of 3.6 grams of pseudoephedrine and ephedrine per day, and 9 grams in a 30-day period. Each mail order purchase is limited to 7.5 grams in a 30-day period.

■ The store staff must record the items and quantity the patient received.

■ The customer must record their name, address, and the date and time of the sale, and sign the logbook. An ID card may be electronically swiped to capture the name and address.

■ The store staff then must verify this information—checking that the photo on the ID matches the customer and that the date and time are correct. Many stores can swipe the driver's license to record the name and address.

The DEA requires that the logbook be kept for at least 2 years. It must be kept secured and the information in it cannot be shared with the public. Inspectors and law enforcement can have access to the logbook. All pharmacy staff members be trained on how to sell pseudoephedrine and ephedrine.

Individual states can choose to have further restrictions, including not selling these products at all, due to widespread abuse in their state.

If your state has further restrictions than those listed above, please list them here:

Dextromethorphan

Dextromethorphan is an OTC cough suppressant commonly found in more than 120 OTC cough and cold medications either as a single agent or in combination with other drugs.

Dextromethorphan is often abused in high doses (especially by teenagers and young adults) to generate euphoria and visual and auditory hallucinations. Illicit use of dextromethorphan is referred to on the street as "Robo-tripping" or "skittling". Dextromethorphan is not currently scheduled under the Controlled Substances Act (CSA). However, the CSA indicated that dextromethorphan may become a scheduled drug in the future. As of August 2015, eight states have prohibited sales of any dextromethorphan-containing product to persons younger than 18 years of age (California, New York, Arizona, Louisiana, Virginia, Tennessee, Kentucky and Washington). If there is an age minimum, proof of age is required.

List your state requirements for selling dextromethorphan:

MEDICAL MARIJUANA

As of the fall of 2015, 23 states and the District of Columbia have legalized marijuana, primarily to treat medical conditions. However, the federal government, at that time, considered marijuana to have no legitimate medical use and it remains classified as a schedule I drug.

On March 10, 2015, three senators introduced a bill that would legalize medical marijuana at the federal level. The bill, known as the Compassionate Access, Research Expansion and Respect States Act (CARERS), would re-classify marijuana from schedule I to schedule II and "allow patients, doctors and businesses in states that have already passed medical marijuana laws to participate in those programs without fear of federal prosecution". Marijuana distribution takes place in marijuana dispensaries, not in pharmacies. Paraphernalia required for marijuana use cannot be sold in pharmacies.

Dispensing Nonprescription Drugs

OTC or nonprescription drugs are considered safe and effective for self-diagnosed conditions by the general public, have adequate written directions for self-use, and do not require physician supervision. No prescription is therefore required for the purchase of OTC products. Pharmacists should be able to determine when it is safe to recommend an OTC product, and when the patient should be referred to an appropriate healthcare provider for further evaluation.

LABELING REQUIREMENTS FOR NONPRESCRIPTION DRUGS

The labeling on prescription drugs is written for healthcare providers. The labeling on OTC drugs is written for patients who may not have medical training. Therefore, the language needs to be written in a manner that a layperson can understand, in order to be able to use the drug safely, and for the purpose/s for which it is intended. If any of the required information listed here is missing, the OTC drug is considered misbranded. The following are required on the labeling of OTC products:[62]

- A principal display panel, which refers to the part of an OTC drug label that is most likely to be displayed or examined in a retail setting. The principal display panel should be large enough to accommodate all the mandatory label information.

- A statement of identity, which refers to the established name of the drug, followed by an accurate statement of the general pharmacological category or the principal intended action of the drug (e.g., chlorpheniramine, antihistamine). The statement of identity should be included on the principal display panel.

- A declaration of the net quantity of contents, which is expressed in the terms of weight, measure, numerical count, or a combination or numerical count and weight, measure, or size.

- The name and address of the manufacturer, packer, or distributor.

---

62 http://www.accessdata.fda.gov/scripts/cdrh/cfdocs/cfCFR/CFRSearch.cfm?CFRPart=201&showFR=1&subpartNode=21:4.0.1.1.2.1

- The National Drug Code (NDC) number is requested, but is not required to appear on all OTC drug labels.

- Adequate directions for use, which includes dosing, preparation, frequency, duration, time, and route of administration.

- "Drug Facts" panel, which is an FDA-approved label used to educate patients. The following table describes the requirements of the Drug Facts panel.

REQUIRED INFORMATION FOR DRUG FACTS PANEL	
Active Ingredient	Active ingredient of drug, including dosage unit and quantity per dose
Purposes	General pharmacological category or principal intended action
Uses	Indications
Warnings	The below warnings must be included when appropriate: • "If pregnant or breast-feeding, ask a health professional before use." OTC drugs are exempt from this warning if it is intended to benefit the fetus or nursing infant during the period of pregnancy or nursing or labeled exclusively for pediatric use (e.g., prenatal vitamins). Orally or rectally administered OTC aspirin and aspirin-containing drug products must bear an additional warning: "It is especially important not to use aspirin during the last 3 months of pregnancy unless definitely directed to do so by a doctor because it may cause problems in the unborn child or complications during delivery." • "For external use only" for topical drug products not intended for ingestion • "For rectal use only" • "For vaginal use only" • "Reye's syndrome" warning for drug products containing salicylates • Allergic reaction and asthma alert warnings • Flammability warning • Choking warning • Liver warning and/or stomach bleeding warning • Sore throat warning • Dosage warning for drug products containing sodium phosphates • Sexually transmitted infections warning for vaginal contraceptive and spermicide drug products containing nonoxynol-9 • "Do not use", followed by all contraindications for use with the product • "Ask a doctor before use if you have" followed by all the conditions in which the product should not be used • "Ask a doctor or pharmacist before use if you are" followed by all drug-drug and drug-food interaction warnings • "When using this product", followed by the side effects that the consumer may experience, and the substances (e.g., alcohol) or activities (e.g., operating machinery, driving a car) to avoid while using the product • "Stop use and ask a doctor if", followed by any signs of toxicity or other reactions that would necessitate immediately discontinuing use of the product • Any other required warnings in an applicable OTC drug monograph, other OTC drug regulations, or approved drug application • "Keep out of reach of children" warning and the accidental overdose/ingestion warning

REQUIRED INFORMATION FOR DRUG FACTS PANEL, CONTINUED	
Directions	Dosage directions for specific age groups or populations
Other Information	Other information that may be required by monograph, regulations, or labeling. This includes information regarding certain ingredients (see following for more information regarding electrolyte labeling): • Sodium labeling • Calcium labeling • Magnesium labeling • Potassium labeling Inactive ingredients (e.g., coloring, flavoring), listed in alphabetical order
Contact Information	"Questions" or "Questions and Comments?" must be stated, followed by the telephone number

OTC LABELING FOR SODIUM, CALCIUM, MAGNESIUM AND POTASSIUM

Federal regulations require the labeling of electrolyte (sodium, calcium, magnesium, potassium) content per dosage unit if it exceeds the threshold amount set by the FDA.[63] If the electrolyte content surpasses the threshold (see table), then the label must have a warning statement informing consumers to ask a doctor before use if the patient has kidney stones/kidney disease or a sodium/calcium/magnesium/potassium restricted diet. The warning statements may be combined, if applicable, provided that the ingredients are listed in alphabetical order (e. g., a calcium or sodium restricted diet).

ELECTROLYTE	TERM/WARNING STATEMENT	THRESHOLD AMOUNT PER DAILY DOSE
Sodium	Sodium Free	≤ 5 mg
	Very Low Sodium	≤ 35 mg
	Low Sodium	≤ 140 mg
	Ask a doctor before use if you have a sodium restricted diet	> 140 mg
Calcium	Each (insert appropriate dosage unit) contains: (insert names of ingredients in alphabetical order and the quantity of each ingredient)	≥ 20 mg
	Ask a doctor before use if you have • kidney stones • calcium-restricted diet	> 3.2 g
Magnesium	Each (insert appropriate dosage unit) contains: (insert names of ingredients in alphabetical order and the quantity of each ingredient)	≥ 8 mg
	Ask a doctor before use if you have • kidney stones • magnesium-restricted diet	> 600 mg
Potassium	Each (insert appropriate dosage unit) contains: (insert names of ingredients in alphabetical order and the quantity of each ingredient)	≥ 5 mg
	Ask a doctor before use if you have • kidney stones • potassium-restricted diet	> 975 mg

63   http://www.accessdata.fda.gov/scripts/cdrh/cfdocs/cfCFR/CFRSearch.cfm?CFRPart=201&showFR=1&subpartNode=21:4.0.1.1.2.3

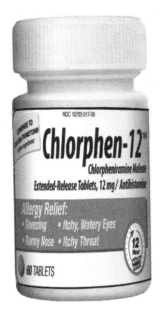

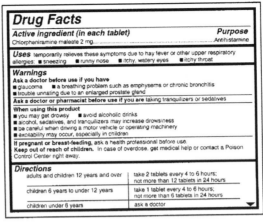

Drug Facts

Active ingredient (in each tablet)	Purpose
Chlorpheniramine maleate 2 mg..	........................Antihistamine

Uses temporarily relieves these symptoms due to hay fever or other upper respiratory allergies: ■ sneezing ■ runny nose ■ itchy, watery eyes ■ itchy throat

Warnings
Ask a doctor before use if you have
■ glaucoma ■ a breathing problem such as emphysema or chronic bronchitis
■ trouble urinating due to an enlarged prostate gland
Ask a doctor or pharmacist before use if you are taking tranquilizers or sedatives
When using this product
■ you may get drowsy ■ avoid alcoholic drinks
■ alcohol, sedatives, and tranquilizers may increase drowsiness
■ be careful when driving a motor vehicle or operating machinery
■ excitability may occur, especially in children
If pregnant or breast-feeding, ask a health professional before use.
Keep out of reach of children. In case of overdose, get medical help or contact a Poison Control Center right away.

Directions

adults and children 12 years and over	take 2 tablets every 4 to 6 hours; not more than 12 tablets in 24 hours
children 6 years to under 12 years	take 1 tablet every 4 to 6 hours; not more than 6 tablets in 24 hours
children under 6 years	ask a doctor

Drug Facts (continued)

Other information ■ store at 20-25°C (68-77°F) ■ protect from excessive moisture

Inactive ingredients D&C yellow no. 10, lactose, magnesium stearate, microcrystalline cellulose, pregelatinized starch

OTC Drug Facts Label

OTC EMERGENCY CONTRACEPTION

Emergency contraception (EC) can prevent pregnancy when taken up to 5 days following unprotected sexual intercourse. There are two FDA-approved EC pills: levonorgestrel (prescription and OTC) and ulipristal (prescription only).[64] *Plan B One-Step* and the generic versions *(Take Action, Next Choice One-Dose,* and *My Way)* are available OTC, with no gender or age requirements. No prescription or identification is required for purchase. Even though the package directions for the generics state that the use is intended for use by women ages 17 and older, anyone can buy these products. The FDA has requested that *Plan B One-Step* and the generics be placed in the aisle with the other family planning items, such as condoms and spermicide. The pharmacy does not need to be open to purchase these products as long as the general store is open. The FDA has approved *Plan B One-Step* and similar products for up to 72 hours after unprotected intercourse, but pharmacists can recommend them up to 120 hours. However, EC is more effective if taken as soon as possible

---

64   http://ec.princeton.edu/get-EC-now.html and http://www.ncsl.org/research/health/emergency-contraception-state-laws.aspx (accessed 2015 Jul 30).

The Affordable Care Act (ACA or Obamacare) will cover women's preventative health services at no cost sharing with a valid prescription, which includes birth control and emergency contraception. This will require a prescription; OTC products are not included with this coverage. In some states, the pharmacist can prescribe emergency contraception independently, or pursuant to a physician directed protocol. Ulipristal (*Ella*) is preferred when it has been 72-120 hours since unprotected intercourse.

Alternatively, a female could use regular birth control pills as emergency contraception if taken in high doses. These are not preferred.

Some women use the copper intrauterine device (IUD) for regular birth control, which is an effective emergency contraceptive if inserted up to 5 days after unprotected sex. As emergency contraception, the copper IUD is more effective than either type of emergency contraceptive pill, reducing risk of getting pregnant by more than 99%. It is not as convenient as taking oral tablets, but the benefit of long-term contraception may be useful.

BEHIND THE COUNTER DRUGS

In addition to prescription and non-prescription drugs, there is a third category of drugs called behind the counter (BTC) drugs. The FDA legally classifies these drugs as OTC, they are typically stored behind the counter so that customers must ask the pharmacist or another staff member to retrieve the drug. The sale may need to be recorded, such as with pseudoephedrine, which requires the identify of the purchaser recorded, and has quantity restrictions. This is discussed further in the Controlled Substances section under The Combat Methamphetamine Epidemic Act.

Some Schedule V drugs, such as codeine containing cough syrups, may be classified as OTC products in a few states. These drugs are sold without a prescription, but are available only when dispensed by a pharmacist. Quantity restrictions, age restrictions, and/or recordkeeping rules may also apply. This is discussed in the Controlled Substances section.

INDEX